C000216125

200 YEARS OF THE
LANCASTER CANAL

AN ILLUSTRATED HISTORY

TO DOROTHY
In memory of many canal visits, on foot and by water.

BY THE SAME AUTHOR

The Canals of North West England (2 vols) with Charles Hadfield, 1970

Victorian Stations, 1973

The British Railway Station ('Railway History in Pictures' series), with Jeoffry Spence, 1977

Pennine Waterway: A pictorial history of the Leeds & Liverpool Canal, 1977

Lancashire Waterways, 1980

Railway Stations in the North West, 1981

The Railway Heritage of Britain, with O.S. Nock, 1983

Great Railway Stations of Britain: their Architecture, Growth and Development, 1986

The Railways around Preston: An Historical Review, 1989, 2nd edition, 1992

The Railway Surveyors: Railway Property Management, 1800 – 1990, 1990

The Oxford Companion to British Railway History, with Jack Simmons (eds) 2003

Britain's Historic Railway Buildings: An Oxford Gazetteer of Structures and Sites, 2003, 2nd revised edition, 2011

Railways in the Landscape: How they transformed the face of Britain, 2016

ILLUSTRATIONS

Except where otherwise acknowledged, all illustrations are by the author or from his collection.

Photographic imaging by Paul Aitken

Maps by Alison Aitken.

200 YEARS OF THE
LANCASTER CANAL

AN ILLUSTRATED HISTORY

GORDON BIDDLE

PEN & SWORD
TRANSPORT

AN IMPRINT OF PEN & SWORD BOOKS LTD.
YORKSHIRE – PHILADELPHIA

First published in Great Britain in 2018 by
PEN & SWORD TRANSPORT

An imprint of Pen & Sword Books Ltd
Yorkshire - Philadelphia

Copyright © Gordon Biddle, 2018

ISBN: 978 1 52670 434 4

The right of Gordon Biddle to be identified as Author of this work has been asserted by him in accordance
with the Copyright, Designs and Patents Act 1988.

A CIP catalogue record for this book is available from the British Library

All rights reserved. No part of this book may be reproduced or transmitted in any form or by any means,
electronic or mechanical including photocopying, recording or by any information storage and retrieval
system, without permission from the Publisher in writing.

Typeset in Palatino 11/13 by
Aura Technology and Software Services, India

Printed and bound in India by Replika Press Pvt. Ltd.

Pen & Sword Books Ltd incorporates the Imprints of Pen & Sword Books Archaeology, Atlas, Aviation,
Battleground, Discovery, Family History, History, Maritime, Military, Naval, Politics, Railways, Select,
Transport, True Crime, Fiction, Frontline Books, Leo Cooper, Praetorian Press, Seaforth Publishing,
Wharncliffe and White Owl.

For a complete list of Pen & Sword titles please contact

PEN & SWORD BOOKS LTD
47 Church Street, Barnsley, South Yorkshire, S70 2AS, England
E-mail: enquiries@pen-and-sword.co.uk
Website: www.pen-and-sword.co.uk

Or
PEN AND SWORD BOOKS
1950 Lawrence Rd, Havertown, PA 19083, USA
E-mail: Uspen-and-sword@casematepublishers.com
Website: www.penandswordbooks.com

CONTENTS

ACKNOWLEDGEMENTS

I have to thank the following for their kind assistance:

John S. Gavan, vice-president, Lancaster Canal Trust.

David Slater, former chairman of the trust, and Frank Sanderson, former publicity officer, for reading and commenting on drafts of Chapter 8.

Mike Clarke, president of the Leeds & Liverpool Canal Society, for valuable additional material.

C.W.N. Crewdson, OBE, chairman of Gilbert Gilkes & Gordon Ltd.

Mr & Mrs P.T.A. Holland of Capernwray Mill.

The late John Freeman, Area Engineer, British Waterways Board.

The late Dan Ashcroft, who was born on a canal boat and with his family lived and worked for most of his life on the canal.

Keith Tassart, who worked on the canal and was an invaluable source of information.

David Berry of Preston, for drawing my attention to the Cragg family diaries.

Wendy Luty, who somehow managed to decipher my handwriting and type the manuscript.

My daughter Alison Aitken, for the maps.

My son-in-law Paul Aitken for painstaking photographic imaging of all the illustrations.

John Scott-Morgan, my editor Carol Trow, and their colleagues at Pen & Sword Books Ltd.

Dr. Bill Fawcett for proofreading.

PREFACE

Although several guides to the Lancaster Canal have been published in the past, primarily aimed at walkers and boat users, there has been no detailed history since I collaborated with Charles Hadfield in the two-volume *Canals of North West England* in his 'Canals of the British Isles' series in 1970. With the approach of the bi-centenary of the canal's completion to Kendal in 2019, and the increasing interest in it, particularly the efforts to re-open to Kendal, now seems an appropriate time to record its long, and at times, uncertain existence. Past research into the canal company's extensive records in the National Archive at Kew (formerly the Public Record Office), the Cumbria County Archive at Kendal and the Lancashire Archives at Preston, together with recent research, form the basis of the story. In the hope of attracting as wide a readership as possible I have deliberately refrained from adopting the customary academic convention of annotations and footnotes to show sources but instead I have mentioned them in the text and included an extensive bibliography.

Gordon Biddle
Spring, 2018

CHAPTER 1

BEGINNINGS

Before the Canal Era

Until the mid-eighteenth century British trade and commerce depended on roads and rivers for transport, or in areas near the sea, coastal shipping. Roads were poor, often only rough tracks, until the first turnpike road of 1683 started a programme of improvements over the next century. Carriage was by pack horse or horse-drawn wagon. Rivers were subject to floods and droughts; coastal sailing craft were dependent on wind and tides, good harbours and, of course, the weather. Passengers travelled on horse-back or by stage-coach, or where possible by river boat or by sea.

In south Lancashire, the principal trading artery was the River Mersey, particularly after 1721 when the Mersey & Irwell Navigation Company began straightening and improving the two rivers between Liverpool and the growing industrial area around Manchester, eventually leading to the opening of the Manchester Ship Canal in 1885.

Further north in the county the River Douglas was progressively made navigable from the mouth of the Ribble estuary to Wigan, principally to carry coal down to the coast and thence to ports in Cheshire, Lancashire and Westmorland, with return cargoes of manufactured goods and imports, mainly from Liverpool, and stone and slate from the north. They were carried in flat-bottomed sailing barges called 'flats', small at first but by the nineteenth century loading up to 100 tons. As well as coastal trading, they went as far as Ireland and the Isle of Man. Their dimensions were largely dictated by the capacity of other navigations in north-west England.

Estuaries

The Ribble estuary was navigable to Preston as early as 1360, but was hindered by shifting sands until a channel was dredged in 1838. On the north bank a shallow creek could take flats to a wharf at Freckleton, opened in 1738, and in 1842 a small dock was opened at Lytham. Later, more improvements were made to the Ribble, culminating in the opening of Preston Dock in 1892, at that time the largest single dock basin in the world.

Further north, the Wyre estuary was navigable to Hambledon and Skippool from at least the mid-1600s to about 1870, when it was finally supplanted by Fleetwood at its mouth. In north Lancashire, the tidal River Lune was navigable to Lancaster, where the Lancaster Port Commission was established by an Act of 1749 and began constructing St. George's Quay. Earlier, about 1700, a jetty was constructed at Sunderland Point on the north bank close to the sea, but it could only be used at high tide. Like the Ribble, the Lune estuary was severely hampered by shifting sands and silting. An attempt to alleviate these difficulties was made when, in 1787, the commissioners opened a dock at Glasson, some five miles south of Lancaster, where there was a deeper channel, but the intervening roads were poor. A further attempt to improve access to Lancaster was made in 1799, when a ship canal was proposed from Thornbush, a mile nearer the sea than Glasson and capable of taking large craft to Lancaster, but although money was raised, it was a time of economic depression and the Port Commission was in debt. The scheme was finally abandoned in 1813. As the size of ships grew, so Lancaster's decline as a port continued.

For sea-going trade, Kendal relied on Milnthorpe, where small craft could penetrate on the tide up the River Beela

Remains of the wharf on Freckleton Creek, 1967.

The Custom House and Warehouse on St George's Quay, Lancaster, 2003.

Glasson Dock in the 1930s, from an old postcard.

Conjectural route of John Longbothom's canal and land reclamation scheme around Morecambe Bay, 1787, see page 13.

for about a mile from the River Kent estuary and Morecambe Bay, together with Sandside and several places on the estuary itself from Arnside to Blackstone Point. Most vessels were beached for loading and unloading into carts on the sands between tides, although several stone quays were built. Others discharged into lighters bound for Milnthorpe. But they, too, were dependent on the tides and subject to changing channels. On the opposite side of the Kent, Meathop and Grange-over-Sands also served Kendal. Outward cargoes were mainly slate, limestone and woollen goods, with Wigan coal from the Douglas as the principal import.

The Canal Mania
The first known navigable artificial waterway in Britain was the Roman Fossdyke in Lincolnshire, although its primary purpose was a drainage channel. It was followed in 1566 by the short Exeter Canal, built to avoid the estuary of the Exe up to the city. It was 1745 before another wholly artificial navigation was attempted; the Newry Canal in Ireland, closely followed by the short St. Helens Canal in 1757, built to take coal from south Lancashire to the Mersey. Eight years later, in 1765, the Duke of Bridgewater opened

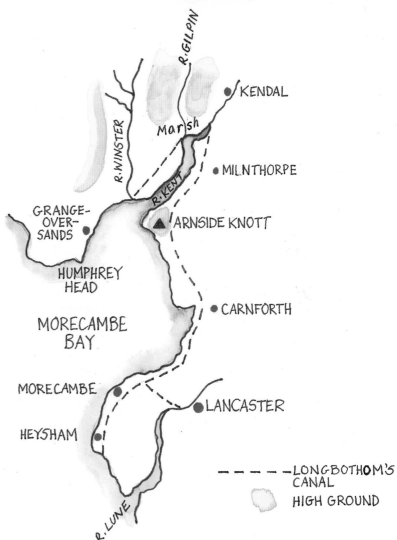

his celebrated canal to convey coal from his mines at Worsley to the rapidly growing industrial towns of Manchester and Salford, extending to the Mersey at Runcorn in 1776.

Industrialisation was growing fast, especially in Lancashire. The Bridgewater Canal clearly showed the superiority of canal transport over roads and rivers; safer, more reliable and, most importantly, faster. Alongside the development of steam power, canals can be said to have begun the real Industrial Revolution as the so-called Canal Mania took hold. By 1840 there were some 4,000 miles of inland navigation in Britain, joining the Mersey, the Humber, the Thames, the Bristol Channel and beyond. After 1840, competition from the new railways began to bite and after about 1850 the canal era entered slow decline.

The canals and river navigations were built by separate companies, of which at the end of the canal era there were over two hundred, in some areas competing with one another. Many canals, especially in the Midlands, were 'narrow', capable of taking craft 70ft long but only 7ft wide, hence the term 'narrowboat'. Others, particularly those connected to rivers, were 'broad', taking wider barges with greater capacity.

Apart from a few trunk routes, most canal companies were local promotions, and in order to build them an Act of Parliament was needed, principally to gain powers to compulsorily purchase land on an approved route. They operated similarly to toll roads, open to independent carriers on payment of a toll that was specified in the Act. Having been authorised by an Act of Parliament, any subsequent changes a canal company wished to make frequently required a further Act. Towards the end of the nineteenth century, several larger canal companies set up their own carrying fleets.

The Canal Mania produced a number of schemes in south Lancashire. The most ambitious was the Leeds & Liverpool, a cross-Pennine waterway aiming to link the navigable River Aire at Leeds, and thence the Humber, with the Mersey. It was incorporated by an Act of 1770 but after many vicissitudes was not completed until 1816. Its projected route from Liverpool through south and east Lancashire lay by way of Ormskirk, Leyland and west of Blackburn to join the Ribble Valley, thence following the Lancashire Calder and Pendle Water to Colne before entering Yorkshire. At Newburgh, near Ormskirk, it was proposed to cross the River Douglas navigation on an aqueduct, but later connected with it in order to gain access to the Wigan coalfield, eventually acquiring it outright. A connection with the Bridgewater Canal near Leigh would link it to projected canals around Manchester, and eventually southward to the Midlands. As we shall see later, the Lancashire section was to change.

The first proposal

Further north, manufacturing and mercantile interests in Preston, Lancaster and Kendal for long had been seeking a reduction in the high price of coal brought down the Douglas to the Ribble estuary and thence to Preston, or around the coast to the Lune or across Morecambe Bay to Milnthorpe. A forerunner of the Leeds & Liverpool was a cross-Pennine 'Grand Canal' scheme of 1766 linking the Ribble with the Aire, and by numerous branches, the Mersey with the Humber, one branch running from Preston to Lancaster. Although Lancaster men had refused to support both it and a 1769 proposal for a canal linking the Bridgewater to Lancaster, they saw that a south-to-north canal from the Leeds & Liverpool could provide the answer for cheaper coal. A return traffic was available in limestone from Westmorland and north Lancashire for burning into lime for mortar in building and for use as an agricultural fertiliser which was in demand in the Fylde and on the west Lancashire plain.

Accordingly, a group of Lancaster merchants took the lead and called a meeting on 13 November 1771, when it was decided to ask the pioneer canal engineer James Brindley to survey a route. But Brindley was too busy, and delegated the work to his assistant, Robert Whitworth, who later made his own name as a canal engineer. It was not an easy route, cutting across the grain of the country, requiring aqueducts over numerous streams and rivers, two of them major; the Ribble and the Lune. They presented obstacles that Whitworth's successors would also encounter.

In the following year, he submitted plans for a canal from the projected Leeds & Liverpool at Eccleston near Chorley to Kendal. It would cross the Ribble below Penwortham Bridge at Preston, then loop westward almost to Kirkham before turning back close to Barton and continuing northward to the Lune, which it crossed below Skerton Bridge at Lancaster, and then forward to Tewitfield, north of Carnforth.

Thus far the canal would be level for 54½ miles before rising 86ft by locks to a further level of 18 miles to Kendal. Large aqueducts would be required to cross the Ribble and the Lune, and a tunnel under Hincaster Hill, five miles from Kendal, in order to serve the Wakefields' gunpowder mills at Sedgwick. Asked to find an easier route with a shorter aqueduct over the Lune, Whitworth responded by suggesting crossing the Ribble by a smaller structure, but needing locks rising 24ft; a shorter westward loop; and another one east of Lancaster to Halton in order to achieve a shorter aqueduct over the Lune. Because this line would be lower, a second set of locks would be required at Tewitfield, rising a further 62 ft. The total distance to Kendal would be increased by only ½ mile, but with eight more locks. Additionally, the canal would not pass as close to Preston and Lancaster as in his original scheme. After that, nothing happened for twenty years.

Other Schemes

However, north of Lancaster other minds were not idle. In 1779, a survey was made for a canal from Ingleton and Burton-in-Lonsdale where there was coal, to the Lune at Conder Green near Lancaster, followed a year later with an extension to Settle. Six years afterwards, in 1787, John Wilkinson, the pioneer ironmaster of Castle Head near Lindale in south Westmorland, enthusiastically proposed a remarkable scheme to enclose and drain 38,710 acres of sand and marsh on the east and north sides of Morecambe Bay and to create a coast-wise canal, using the excavated material to form an embankment. The idea appears to have originated from John Jenkinson of Yealand. John Longbothom, the first engineer of the Leeds & Liverpool Canal, was asked to survey. He went further and proposed that, in addition, the River Winster should be diverted into an artificial channel from the point where it entered the Kent estuary near Castle Head across Foulshaw Moss to rejoin the Kent near Nether Levens. From there the Kent itself would be diverted into a second coast-wise channel to Arnside, from where it would cut across country behind Arnside Knott to Warton Crag. There it would rejoin the coast and pass close to the present-day Carnforth and Morecambe to deep sea at Heysham Head; an ambitious scheme of some 24 miles, which Longbothom costed at £150,000, see map on page 11. In addition to reclaiming extensive areas of Morecambe Bay, he pointed out that the channel could be navigable from the Kent to Bare – now part of Morecambe – from where a short canal could be cut for about three miles to the Lune at Lancaster, thereby simultaneously providing easily navigable water from the sea to Lancaster avoiding the shallow Lune, reviving Lancaster as a port, and creating navigable water to within six miles of Kendal. Wilkinson offered to invest £50,000, while Jenkinson, in seeking support from Lord George Cavendish of Holker Hall, went on to suggest that it would be easy to build a branch canal to Kendal itself. Apparently neither Jenkinson nor Wilkinson were able to convince his lordship, as no more seems to have been heard of the scheme.

During this period, leading Lancaster citizens were becoming increasingly vocal for a canal from the south, now considered a necessity if the city was to compete with growing towns south of the Ribble. On 8 June 1791, at a meeting called by the mayor, it was resolved to promote a waterway and seek public subscriptions to a company. A committee was formed, with Samuel Gregson as clerk. Gregson (1762-1846) was a leading Lancaster merchant and twice mayor.

Obtaining an Act

The committee's first move was to ask Robert Dickinson, Richard Beck – both engineers – and Longbothom to try to improve on Whitworth's route,

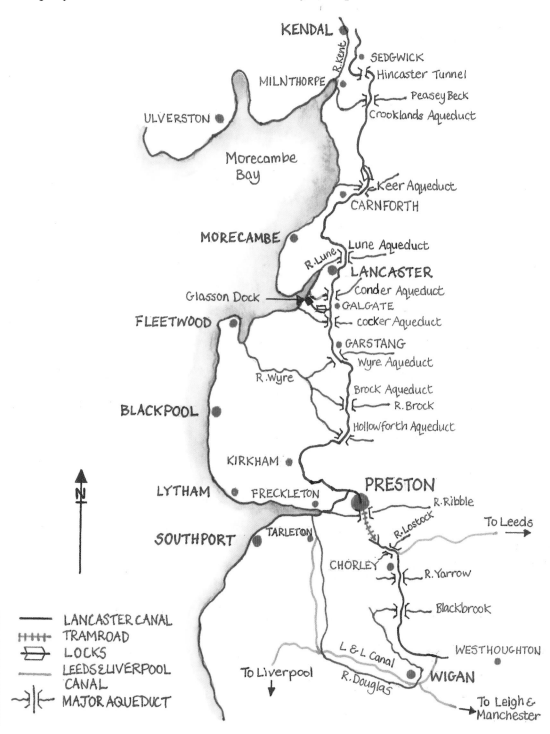

The Lancaster Canal as built.

and to extend the southern end to the Bridgewater Canal at Worsley. They could not find a better one, so the committee, determined to seek an alternative, resolved to approach John Rennie, an engineer gaining a high reputation. Although only 30, he had completed a number of important projects, and went on to build the London and East India Docks, the Bell Rock Lighthouse and, best known, the second London Bridge, among many others. He was probably the most prolific of British civil engineers. His sons George and John Jr, were also engineers.

In January 1792 Rennie produced a revised scheme for a canal wide enough to take Mersey flats, running from Westhoughton, in the mining area between Wigan and Bolton, for 15½ miles to Clayton Green, south of Preston. There it would descend 222ft into the Ribble valley, requiring 32 locks, followed by an aqueduct over the river. Thereafter Rennie kept to Whitworth's first route to Tewitfield, with a short deviation at Lancaster to cross the Lune further downstream, 42½ miles on the level. He then took a more direct course to Hincaster, requiring only five locks at Tewitfield but four more at Millness, near Crooklands, after which he maintained Whitworth's route to Kendal, a total of 75½ miles from Westhoughton. He added a 3-mile branch from near Chorley to pits at Duxbury, and one of 2½ miles from Tewitfield to limestone quarries at Warton Crag. In total, there would be about 225 road bridges and 22 aqueducts. The committee immediately promoted a Parliamentary Bill. The main promoters were the Earl of Crawford and Balcarres, a prominent coalowner of Haigh Hall near Wigan; John Brockbank, a Lancaster shipbuilder; John Dilworth and Thomas Worswick, Lancaster bankers; John Wakefield and Thomas Crewdson, Kendal bankers; other leading citizens of Lancaster and Kendal; Edmund Rigby of Liverpool; and Robert and Bold Hesketh-Fleetwood from the powerful Fylde family.

Quarrels with the Leeds & Liverpool

During this period, the Leeds & Liverpool Canal had acquired the River Douglas Navigation which, it will be remembered, was planned to be crossed by an aqueduct near Newburgh. To avoid this, the Leeds & Liverpool decided to adopt a new route away from the Ribble valley and Preston, serving the rapidly growing east Lancashire cotton towns of Colne, Burnley, Accrington, Blackburn and Chorley to Wigan, then using the Douglas to Newburgh where it would regain its original route to Liverpool. It was somewhat longer, but would certainly be more lucrative. Between Chorley and Wigan, it would be parallel to Rennie's route for the Lancaster – at one point only 100yd away – which would not only tap into the Lancaster's potential traffic but would intercept agreed water supplies from drainage from neighbouring pits, a number of them owned by Earl Balcarres. Lord Derby, another prominent coal owner, was also a strong supporter of the Lancaster. Further, the recently authorised Manchester Bolton & Bury Canal was seeking to extend from Bolton to join the Leeds & Liverpool at Red Moss, near Horwich, giving it access to Liverpool and, again, depriving the Lancaster of traffic. An agreement was quickly reached with the Manchester Bolton & Bury, but relations with the Leeds & Liverpool deteriorated, entering a period of acrimonious political and parliamentary argument and jockeying for position.

In 1792, the Lancaster's Bill was before parliament seeking incorporation, with powerful support that included the Duke of Bridgewater who saw the proposed connection with his own canal as a northern outlet for his coal. The Leeds & Liverpool suggested that south of Preston the Lancaster should join its new line instead of keeping to Rennie's, but the Lancaster had the stronger support, although at one point overtures by the Leeds & Liverpool to the Earl of Balcarres had to be countered by reminding his lordship of the agreement to help develop his mines by taking drainage water for the canal. Parliamentary opposition from the Leeds & Liverpool was overcome and the Lancaster succeeded in gaining its Act of Incorporation on 24 June. It authorised Rennie's line, including the Duxbury and Warton Crag branches and, as late additions, junctions with projected canals from Ingleton and Hornby, Kirkby Lonsdale and places in the Fylde area. The River Mint at Kendal was to provide the main water supply. However, the Leeds & Liverpool persisted, introducing a Bill for its east Lancashire deviation in the next parliamentary session, 1793, only to be defeated. The Lancaster was now in a strong position and work was quickly started. The Leeds & Liverpool on the other hand, had a route they no longer wanted but could not gain authorisation for an alternative. Arguments between the two companies continued for a year, until in April 1794 they reached a compromise. The Lancaster agreed to support the Manchester Bolton & Bury's Red Moss extension Bill, which the Leeds & Liverpool wanted, if the Leeds & Liverpool in return would support a Lancaster Bill for a small deviation at Cabus near Garstang. Both parties accepted that there would be two parallel canals south of Preston, and the Lancaster undertook to make a short connecting link at Heapey, between Blackburn and Chorley. In the event, the Lancaster lost its Bill, while the Leeds & Liverpool's re-introduced Bill for its east Lancashire deviation was passed in May. There the matter rested until 1810. As for the Manchester Bolton & Bury's attempts to reach Red Moss, they never succeeded.

Also in 1792, a short canal was promoted from the Leven estuary at the head of Morecambe Bay to the town of Ulverston. It was supported by the Lancaster, which agreed to coal being carried across the bay between the two canals free of duty. The Ulverston Canal gained its Act in 1793, which recognised also that a physical connection might be made between the two canals, although it never happened.

Raising the money

The Lancaster's Act authorised a capital of £414,000 in £100 shares, out of which £60,000 was reserved for the canal in Westmorland, suggesting fears that Lancaster interests might become too dominant, which indeed turned out to be the case. An additional £200,000 could be raised by mortgaging the tolls or by creating additional shares, if required. A maximum toll of 2s.3d (11p) per ton was imposed on coal going through the locks at Preston from a point north of Chorley; elsewhere it was 1½d per mile.

CHAPTER 2

CONSTRUCTION BEGINS

Contracts are placed

As soon as the company was incorporated a committee of management was formed, or board of directors as it would be known today. It was composed of Lancaster men, apart from one each from Preston and Kendal. Dilworth and Worswick were respectively chairman and treasurer, Gregson was appointed clerk – or secretary in today's terms – at a salary of £250 a year plus expenses in travelling, of which he did a lot. Rennie was the engineer at £600 per year on the understanding that he gave five months to on-site supervision, or more if necessary. William Crosley and Archibald Millar were appointed assistant surveyors and, a year later, Millar became resident engineer at £400 a year. He was responsible for the day-to-day superintendence and had previously worked on the Forth & Clyde Canal.

By the end of 1792 a contract for the first phase of construction, from Ellel south of Lancaster, to Tewitfield some twelve miles north of the city, had been placed with John Pinkerton from a well-known family of canal contractors, jointly with John Murray of Colne. Early in the next year they were awarded a second one, from Ellel southward to near Catterall, in total 27 miles. South of the Ribble, a third contract was placed with Paul Vickers of Thorne, near Doncaster, for about eight miles from Chorley to a point above Wigan where the top lock now is. This was an attempt to forestall the Leeds & Liverpool, as we have already seen in the preceding chapter.

1793 was an eventful year. In January at the first shareholders' annual meeting,

it was decided to build a branch canal to Glasson Dock, largely at the insistence of the Lancaster members. Gregson moved quickly to gain an Act in May. The Leeds & Liverpool used it as an opportunity to have a clause inserted restricting the taking of drainage water from mines in the disputed area near Chorley, otherwise the Lancaster was free to use mine water provided it did not require pumping. The following year, in conclusion of negotiations with the Duke of Bridgewater, a further Bill was promoted to extend southward from Westhoughton to his canal at Worsley, but it was lost largely due to opposition from a local landowner. Instead, the duke decided to build a branch from the Bridgewater Canal to Leigh where the Lancaster could meet it.

Where possible, embankments were raised with earth carted from cuttings or, if work between them was sufficiently advanced, by boats. Otherwise spoil had to be dug from neighbouring fields. The Lune embankment, for instance, was made from material from Ashton cutting south of Lancaster and taken by boat.

In 1794, Henry Eastburn, who had worked on the Basingstoke Canal, was engaged as resident engineer for the canal south of the Ribble, with Thomas Fletcher as his assistant. North of it Millar had trouble with Pinkerton and Murray, whose performance had been causing him concern for some time. He complained that they ignored his instructions and that their work was unsatisfactory, particularly their masonry, the quarrying of stone, damage to neighbouring properties and poor puddling work on the bed of the canal. At one point Gregson in despair called on Rennie for help. Their contracts were valued at £52,000 and Robert Whitworth was brought in to arbitrate. In the autumn of 1795 they were discharged and the company took the work into its own hands. At the same time, Pinkerton and Murray voluntarily gave up their contract to construct the Ulverston Canal, citing shortage of money. Gregson and the committee realised that it had been a mistake to divide the Lancaster work into two large contracts, which Millar had not wanted anyway, so they were re-let in short sections. About 1000 men were then working on the canal, employed by thirty-five contractors of varying sizes, one with only two men. By mid-1796 work south of the Ribble had progressed sufficiently to allow some coal traffic to begin, producing much-needed income. The war with France had caused national economic difficulties and money was short. Some shareholders had been ignoring calls on their shares, and the company had been forced to borrow from the treasurer's bank. More money had to be spent on obtaining a third Act in May to authorise a small deviation at Myerscough, near Garstang, and in the following year a second appeal was made to shareholders, fortunately with more success. At the same time, there was growing discontent among the Westmorland shareholders when it was proposed that some of the £60,000 capital allocated in the Act of Incorporation for work within the county should be used to ease the financial situation.

The Lune Aqueduct

By now the canal north of the Ribble was almost completed, only the Lune aqueduct remaining to be finished. Designed by Rennie, it was a mighty work, 600ft long and 50ft high on five 70ft diameter semi-circular arches, beneath a heavy cornice and an elegant balustraded parapet. In the opinion of Dr Cyril T.G Boucher, Rennie's biographer, it is 'possibly the finest bridge in the country'. To save money, Rennie had advocated brick construction, but the

committee would have none of it. Stone was the traditional building material in the district and brick was considered inferior, a view also taken a few years later at Hincaster Tunnel. It was decided to use direct labour to construct the foundations of the piers up to water level, but to let out the superstructure to contractors. In January 1794, William Cartwright was appointed assistant resident engineer under Millar, with special responsibility for the work. Pile-driving began, operated manually, and by July 150 men were at work, 24 hours a day. The piles were 30ft deep, of Baltic pine specially imported from Russia for its durability. Coffer dams were sunk into the river, kept dry by pumps operated by a series of wooden beams from a steam engine and boiler on the south bank. A wooden building was built next to it, using spare timber from the piling, for use as workshops and rather primitive living quarters for the site foreman, Exley, who was paid £250 a year. Life for Cartwright and Exley was difficult. There were frequent labour problems, not helped by large-scale desertions at harvest time; bad weather slowed down work; there were frequent floodings of the works; and pump-men in particular seemed to be frequently drunk. Even so, the foundations and piers were finished within eighteen months, a remarkable achievement, and in recognition Cartwright was presented with a silver cup as a reward for his efforts. In July 1795 the committee proudly reported to a general meeting of shareholders:

'Although the cost has been considerable the Committee trust that succeeding ages will give credit and have reason to boast of the permanency of that Work'.

The contract for the superstructure was awarded to Alexander Stevens and Son of Glasgow. Rennie recommended extra strengthening of the arches but Stevens senior considered them unnecessary. The committee agreed and the relatively

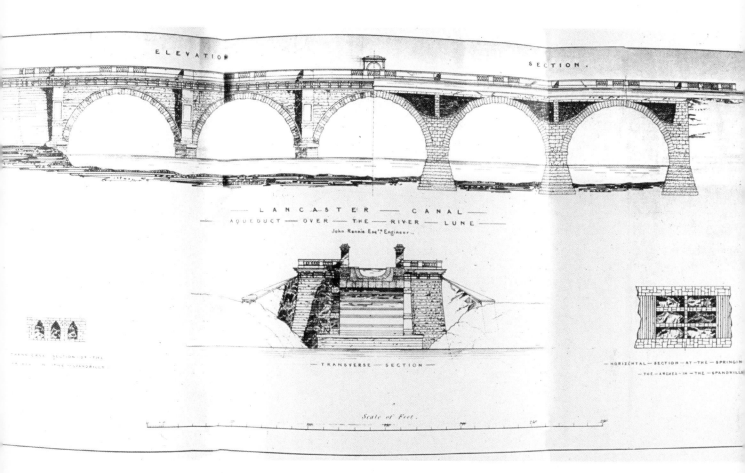

In 1837 S.C. Brees thought construction of the Lune Aqueduct sufficiently impressive to include it in his *Railway Practice*.

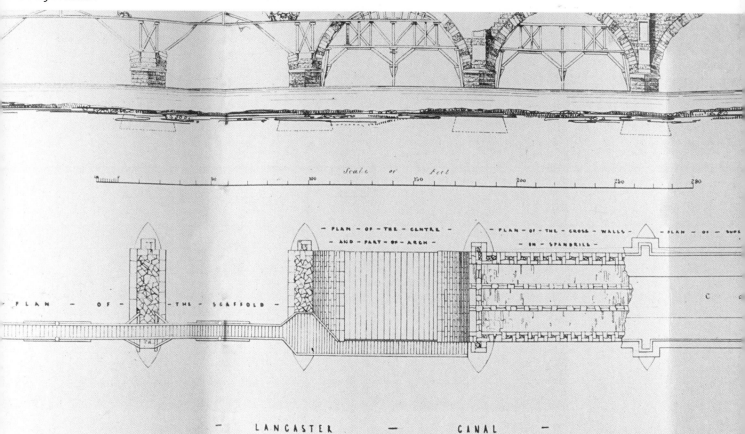

Arches and piers of the aqueduct, 1969.

Looking north along the top, 1969.

The Lune aqueduct
seen from downriver,
1980.

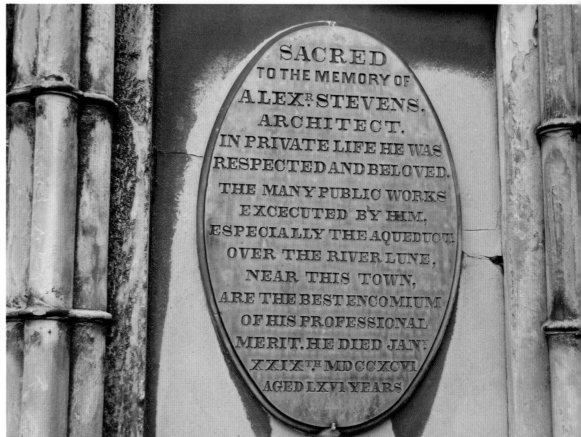

Memorial to
Alexander Stevens on
south wall of Lancaster
Priory church at
Lancaster.

SACRED
TO THE MEMORY OF
ALEXᴿ STEVENS.
ARCHITECT.
IN PRIVATE LIFE HE WAS
RESPECTED AND BELOVED.
THE MANY PUBLIC WORKS
EXECUTED BY HIM,
ESPECIALLY THE AQUEDUCT
OVER THE RIVER LUNE,
NEAR THIS TOWN,
ARE THE BEST ENCOMIUM
OF HIS PROFESSIONAL
MERIT. HE DIED JANʸ
XXIXᵀᴴ MDCCXCVI
AGED LXVI YEARS

little work that has been needed on the aqueduct ever since has proved that he was right, although he did not live to see it completed, dying in January 1796.

He was held in high regard by Rennie and Millar, both of whom paid tribute to his work, which was completed by his son in the following autumn. A noble structure, it demonstrates Rennie's ability to combine sound engineering principles with fine architecture. It had cost £48,321, part of a total of £269,406 spent on the canal to that date. Over each side of the central arch there is a large plaque bearing an inscription. One reads 'To public prosperity'; the other is longer, in Latin, which translated reads:

'Old needs are served, far distant sites combined: Rivers by art to bring new wealth are joined, A.D.1797 J Rennie engineer; A. Stevens & Son, contractors'

Although the drawings in the National Archive clearly bear Rennie's name, there can be confusion over his role and that of the Stevens, father and son, doubtless because there was a contemporary Scottish architect Alexander Stevens of Edinburgh who, Howard Colvin states in his *Biographical Dictionary of British Architects* (1978), 'should not be confused with Alexander Stevens the bridge builder'. Moreover, Stevens' memorial on the outside of the south wall of Lancaster Priory church refers to him as 'architect', and commemorates 'the many public works erected by him especially the aqueduct.' At that time, there was not the same distinction between the professions as today, and some architects still acted as contractors. However, it is quite possible that Stevens may have been responsible for assisting in some of the architectural detailing during the course of construction.

Other aqueducts
Rennie also designed a handsome three-arched aqueduct to cross the Ribble not dissimilar to his Lune aqueduct but, as we shall see, it was never built. His smaller ones, however, still stand, their arches slightly curved in plan to withstand the horizontal thrust of the canal. South of the Ribble, the canal crossed the rivers Douglas and Yarrow, and Black Brook. In 1869 at Red Rock an acutely skewed aqueduct was built by the Lancashire Union Railway over its new line, closed in 1966. In Preston, Tulketh aqueduct crossed the appropriately-named Aqueduct Street on a tall, narrow arch (now demolished) just south of Ashton Basin where the canal now ends. At the northern edge of the city, Savick aqueduct crosses the brook of that name. Further on, Woodplumpton aqueduct has a very low arch just above the level of the brook. Hollowforth is unusual in effectively being three broad circular stone tubes. At Brock, the River Brock presented a problem in being almost level with the canal, which Rennie ingeniously solved by dropping the river over a weir upstream of the aqueduct and deepening it for some distance on the other side. The single arch is a flattened ellipse set between wing walls boat-shaped in plan, beneath a broad parapet.

Rennie developed this principle at the River Calder aqueduct near Catterall, where the disparity in water levels was even less. There he ingeniously dropped the river over a weir into a tunnel that for part of the time is completely submerged, acting as a syphon. Aqueducts over the River Cocker near Forton, the Conder at Galgate and Burrow Beck at the end of Burrow Heights Cutting are built on a similar principle. North of Tewitfield, later on, Thomas Fletcher, Rennie's successor, adopted the same at Farleton.

Next to the Lune, the Wyre aqueduct near Garstang is the largest and most elegant of Rennie's smaller works, a broad 34ft semi-elliptical arch between matching elliptical spandrel walls, surmounted by a dentilled cornice and parapet. Beyond Lancaster, the squat, segmental-arched Bulk aqueduct over Caton Road, adjacent to the Lune, was replaced by a concrete structure in 1966 as part of a road-widening scheme that involved erecting a gantry to carry boats across the road on a cradle while the work was in progress, and a 2ft 6in diameter pipe to carry canal water.

River Lostock on the South End near Whittle-le-Woods, 1968.

Tulketh Aqueduct, Preston, before demolition, 1963.

Savick Aqueduct, Preston, 1971.

Woodplumpton Aqueduct.

Hollowforth Aqueduct, near Barton, 1980.

Brock Aqueduct, 1969.

River Calder Aqueduct and syphon, Catterall, 1980.

River Wyre Aqueduct, Garstang, 1968.

River Conder Aqueduct and syphon, Galgate, 1985.

River Keer Aqueduct, Capernwray, 1968.

Deep Cutting Bridge, Ashton, south of Lancaster, in the early 1900s. (*courtesy Lancaster City Museum*)

Carr Lane or Broken Back Bridge at the north end of Ashton Cutting, near Lancaster, from an old postcard.

The last aqueduct before Tewitfield is over the River Keer at Capernwray, a 35ft tall semi-circular arch set between curved wing walls in a high embankment. One wall contains a pipe passing under the canal bed, which discharged water from upstream on to the overshot wheel of a former corn mill immediately alongside. There was a mill on this site as long ago as 1640, but by 1946 it was being used as a saw mill before being converted into a dwelling in about 1972 – see Chapter 8. The embankment at Stainton was high enough to allow a conventional arch over the beck. Two roads are crossed by tunnel-like aqueducts at Burton-in-Kendal and a third at Sedgwick.

Rennie designed a series of standard bridges carrying roads over the canal, many of them steeply hump-backed. Built in local stone, they are plain and simple, with semi-elliptical arches. By their very simplicity they fit unobtrusively into their localities, seemingly growing out of the landscape. Rennie used a similar design on many of his canals.

The first opening

On 22 November 1797, the canal from Preston, near the present Ashton Basin, to Tewitfield was officially declared open. The committee and local dignitaries sailed in a procession of six boats from Lancaster to the Lune aqueduct, accompanied by an escort from the militia and a barge loaded with limestone. On returning to Lancaster, the flotilla was greeted by an artillery salute, and then carried on to Galgate where it met a northbound barge of coal. After a symbolic exchange of cargo boxes, the party returned to Lancaster and proceeded in procession to the King's Arms for a celebratory dinner.

Shortly afterwards, the Cragg family diary – copied in Lancashire County Archives at Preston – noted that coal was being brought along the canal to Garstang and Lancaster from Savok on the Ribble below Preston. Savok or Savick, from which the brook takes its name, are old spellings for Salwick, where there was a wharf next to Wilson's Bridge. Its main purpose was to serve the small town of Kirkham, some three miles away by road, but could also have been the transfer point for coal brought down the Douglas to the Ribble, which today is within two miles but at that time was nearer, from where it could have been transported by cart to the canal.

By February 1798, the canal south of the Ribble was open from Bark Hill, above Wigan, to Knowley, near Chorley, having so far cost a total of £382,565. Two short arms into Haigh Park – now gone – were built for Earl Balcarres. The two sections of canal now became officially known as the South End and the North End. By this time the company's finances had become precarious, and in July there was only £6,500 in the bank, although growing traffic receipts were starting to provide encouraging income. Meanwhile, Millar and Eastburn's contracts had expired and Cartwright took over responsibility for the whole canal as resident engineer. In October the committee, ever enterprising, started a passenger service with two packet boats between Preston and Lancaster, taking about six hours. Although there was competition from stage coaches, the canal provided a much smoother and more comfortable journey.

Limekilns began to be erected adjacent to both ends of the canal, including some near the Preston terminus by Samuel Gregson & Co., a company formed by Gregson and three fellow directors, or committee-men as they were called. The effect of the canal on Preston's economy was greater than on Lancaster's. William Shakeshaft's map of 1822 shows industrial development and housing on the east side of the canal at Preston, including two waterside cotton mills. Others followed, for all of which the canal provided not only transport but water for their steam engines as well. Preston rapidly expanded into an important industrial town. Lancaster, on the other hand, despite some new industries, largely remained as the historic county town, its economy mainly continuing to centre on the port, although the opening of the Glasson Dock branch canal in 1826 hastened its demise.

Haigh Hall Bridge over the former arm into Haigh Hall Park, near Wigan, c1885. (*courtesy Accrington Library*)

The same bridge in 1980, with date engraved in the keystone.

HAIGH BRIDGE WIGAN

The ornamental Haigh Park bridge over the main canal, c1885. (*courtesy Accrington Library*)

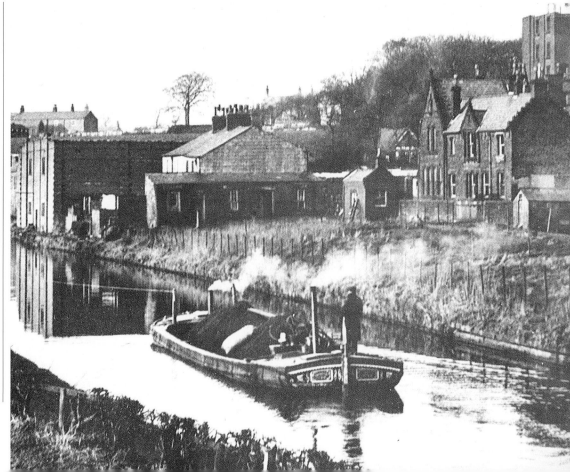

A Leeds & Liverpool horse-drawn barge close to Whittle Springs Brewery on the approach to Johnson's Hillock Locks, 1938. (*courtesy Bolton Evening News*)

Moss Lane bridge and basin close to the foot of Johnson's Hillock Locks, 1968.

CHAPTER 3

CROSSING THE RIBBLE

A year after the official opening, 1799, the South End had been extended a further 1½ miles northward from Chorley to Johnson's Hillock. By this time concern was being felt about how best to join the two ends of the canal, now only eight miles apart. Northbound goods and coal had to be carried by road from the canal at Knowley, near Chorley, to the Douglas, by boat to the Ribble and Freckleton, on up the estuary to Preston, and thence by road again to the North End. So Cartwright was asked to examine the problem. In 1796 and 1797 two proposals had been put forward, one for an inclined plane and branch canal from the Ribble opposite the Douglas outfall to the North End at Salwick, and the other for a tramroad from the Ribble at Preston to the canal terminus at Ashton. The Leeds & Liverpool had agreed to improve the Douglas Navigation, which they eventually did anyway, but the Lancaster had been unable to find the money for its part of the schemes.

Aqueduct versus tramroad

Cartwright costed Rennie's scheme for locks, an embankment and a Ribble aqueduct at £172,945. As an alternative, temporary expedient, he recommended a tramroad to connect the two ends, including canal extensions from the northern terminus to Avenham in Preston, overlooking the Ribble Valley, and on the South End from Johnson's Hillock to Walton Summit, on the south side of the valley. Now a 'Mr Monk', who was James Monk, a Leeds & Liverpool committee-man, submitted a proposal to extend the Douglas Navigation along

the south bank of the Ribble estuary to Penwortham, opposite Preston, there to descend to the river by locks, and on the opposite side an inclined plane up to the North End of the Lancaster. The South End would need a connection to the Leeds & Liverpool at Wigan. Obviously, he saw his plan as a means of extra revenue for the cash-strapped Leeds & Liverpool, estimating that only four more hours would be needed for the journey than by Cartwright's proposed tramroad. But the Lancaster committee rejected it, several coal-owning members from the Chorley and Wigan areas saying that it would cost £54,100 in the first year and £10,750 annually thereafter. One, Alexander Haliburton of Haigh, called the proposal 'insidious'.

Other shareholders were sceptical of the tramroad idea, so the committee asked Rennie and William Jessop, another noted canal engineer, to comment on both proposals and to give their opinions on the merits of crossing the Ribble by either an embankment and aqueduct or entirely by one long aqueduct. In July 1801 they reported to the annual general meeting. They said, 'we are still of the opinion that an embankment the full height of the Lancaster level, and a stone aqueduct will be the most advisable,' including locks down from the South End. They went on to say:

'… on estimating the expense of a design which Mr Rennie has made for an aqueduct of three arches of 116 feet span each, we have no doubt of its being done for less than £94,979. As this sum is not within the Company's funds at present … it will be in the interests of the Company that a temporary mode of conveyance

be immediately adopted, and we know of none more advantageous than by an Iron Rail-way etc.'

Designs for an aqueduct

Rennie's original design was a powerful composition, the three arches being set between heavy piers with prominently stepped buttresses and terminating at curved wing walls. The four end-piers were each surmounted by a tapered obelisk. A plain parapet surmounted a heavily-dentilled cornice. Working with Jessop, Rennie now proposed a less elaborate design, 640ft long and 57ft high from low water to the towing path. Their estimate was little more than half of Cartwright's own design with three 120ft spans decorated with Corinthian pilasters. Thomas Gibson also produced a more elaborate design for a continuous aqueduct across the whole valley, with Gothic-style pointed arches, three of them over the river, with cross-arches within the piers and topped by a huge pediment. It would have been very expensive and appears to have been dismissed out of hand. Had the Ribble been crossed by an aqueduct, the Lancaster would have been notable for two large handsome structures within 34 miles. Monk's proposals were simply dismissed as being of greater benefit to the Leeds & Liverpool than the Lancaster. The two engineers estimated the cost of Cartwright's tramroad at £21,600.

A tramroad is authorised

The committee wasted no time in authorising the tramroad's construction, and Jessop was retained to survey a route through Preston. He was paid £70, and Rennie £112.5s.4d (£112 26.5p). Work began immediately, including extending the South End of the canal northward to Walton Summit, some seven miles, including a 259yd long tunnel at Whittle Hills which proved to be more difficult than was anticipated, and an aqueduct in a tall embankment at the River Lostock. Also, the North End of the canal had to

be extended by about ¾ mile southward into Preston, terminating at a basin just north of Fishergate. Consequently, it was two years before, on 1 June 1803, barges could reach the Summit and transfer their cargoes to tramroad wagons. Even then the tramroad was finished only as far as Bamber Bridge; it was late in the year before it was open to Preston.

Cartwright's plan was for a double-track tramroad as close as possible to the parliamentary line of the canal, with only slight deviations to ease sharp curves and to preserve even gradients. From Walton Summit, the northbound line would descend 215ft on a single gradient, including a short tunnel, to Carr Wood at Penwortham, while a separate southbound line would comprise three level stretches linked by two cable-operated inclined planes, one near Bamber Bridge and the other rising to Walton. From Penwortham, they ran parallel in the conventional manner for ½ mile on a 7ft embankment to a bridge over the Ribble, from where they would rise steeply on another inclined plane to Avenham, the point to which the canal's North End would be further extended from Fishergate. Cartwright proposed a track gauge of 4ft1½in, to carry 2ft deep wagons 6ft by 4ft, each weighing 10cwt. They would cost £14 apiece.

However, Rennie and Jessop advocated a conventional double track over the whole distance, keeping strictly to the parliamentary line of the canal, with three inclined planes at Walton, Penwortham and Avenham. The last would be worked by a steam winding engine and endless chain, but the other two possibly on the self-acting principle whereby ascending wagons were counter-balanced by descending ones. However, their estimate of £21,600 provided for three stationary steam engines; evidently, they were not confident about self-acting inclines.

To raise money for the tramroad, it was proposed to issue new £30 shares, but legal advice was that this would not be permitted under the 1792 Act, meaning that more money had to be spent in obtaining another Act, secured on 20 June 1800. Even then the committee had overlooked that the original Act provided only for a canal, but obviously this was considered to be of no immediate importance and it was 1807 before the tramroad was made legal by the insertion of a clause in a further Act of that year for deviations north of Tewitfield, also authorising 'railways or waggonways within the line of the canal'.

While all this was going on there was more trouble with shareholders, who had divided into three main groups: the original Lancaster promoters anxious to increase the town's trade; a Westmorland party who wanted cheaper coal to Kendal and beyond; and a 'Liverpool Party' of financiers who were prominent investors in many canal promotions and, later, railways. The last group, which included some Preston shareholders, viewed the tramroad as likely to delay a Ribble aqueduct even further, pointing out that the costly aqueduct over the Lune was relatively little used, most of the traffic being to and from Lancaster. In a letter to Gregson, Rennie emphasised that a tramroad should be regarded only as a temporary measure, otherwise it would become an encumbrance, which it did. Gregson assured a dissident shareholder that the tramroad was purely a temporary expedient to speed up traffic and encourage the opening of new mines on the South End. It would also be invaluable, he said, in conveying materials for building the Ribble aqueduct.

Whittle Hills north tunnel, 1953, (see page 101) on what became the Leeds and Liverpool's Walton Summit branch.

The southernmost tunnel at Whittle Hills.

Lime kiln at Rip Row, 1968.

Canal cottage at Rip Row, 1968.

A Leeds & Liverpool
type mile post at
Radburn Wharf, 1968.

Remains of the mordant works at Rip Row, 1968.

Radburn Wharf and basin, 1968.

A reminder of the days of railway ownership; a North Union Railway iron boundary post at Walton Summit, 1963.

Walton Summit bridge, 1968.

Cartwright was sent to Derbyshire to observe the working of the Peak Forest Canal's tramroad, while Gregson was busy buying land. On his return, Cartwright recommended that instead of extending the canal at Preston southward to Avenham, the tramroad should continue northward to meet the canal at its new Fishergate terminus, where the company had already built wharves and warehouses. It would require a short tunnel under Fishergate itself, which would only require a single line

and therefore be cheaper to build. The committee agreed and work began.

Building the tramroad

It seems that Cartwright slightly amended the gauge to 4ft 1in. The rails, or tramplates as they were called, were L-shaped in section, laid with the vertical flanges facing inward to keep the flangeless wagon wheels on the track. They were 3ft long, 3½in wide with 2in high flanges, bowed upward to 3in at the centre, and a 1½in deep rib on the underside. Made of cast iron, they weighed 40lb per yard. Recesses were cast in each end to form a hole where two plates were butted together, through which they were secured to stone sleeper blocks by iron spikes. The blocks came from quarries near Lancaster and were 16-20in long, 12in wide and 8-10in thick, with a hole for the spike filled with a wooden plug. They cost 5d (2.1p) each, and by May 1803, 10,500 had been delivered. Three hundred tons of tramplates were supplied by the Aberdare Ironworks in South Wales at £10.10s (£10.50) per ton, with a reserve on 100 tons more if they proved to be satisfactory. The next lowest tender was from Shelf Ironworks near Bradford, who were told they could have an order for 100 tons if they charged a price of £10.15s per ton (£10.75), to which they agreed. The South End had now been extended to Walton Summit, basins had been made and the incline roadbed was ready, for which Cartwright was instructed to order a steam winding engine and endless chain. Two more were ordered for the Penwortham and Avenham inclines. The engines had 13in cylinders developing 6 horse-power, by Wilkinson of Wrexham, and cost £350 each. Winding wheels, rollers and gear cost £450.

Delay was caused by late delivery from Shelf and defective tramplates from Aberdare. They were 8lb over-weight and broke under a 3½ tons test load. Cartwright wrote to Gregson:

'I confess if they had been moulded in gravel they could not have been rougher handled and the metal of itself is the worst I ever saw, a specimen (six) of which I send you to lay before the committee'.

They were rejected and fresh tenders were sought, Bowling Ironworks near Bradford being awarded an order for 100 tons at £10.15s per ton. The roadbed was now finished, including a wooden trestle bridge over the Ribble at the foot of the Avenham incline and 1,400yd of sidings – Cartwright called them 'splice roads'. Wharves had been established at various places, using some of the inferior tramplates. Extra strong plates were used at level crossings.

At Walton Summit the canal split into three parallel basins, with tramroad tracks between them, the central basin being covered by a two-bay roof. The incline immediately followed, and the winding engine was at its foot; perfectly feasible, of course, with an endless chain which went round a large wheel at the top. The canal called the northbound line the 'coal or descending road' and the southbound the 'limestone or ascending road', based on the principal traffics.

Carr Wood, or Penwortham incline was 165yd long; much the steepest was Avenham, 115yd long at 1 in 6. The engine house was at the top and the lower wheel was on the end of the Ribble bridge. Each incline had a horse-path alongside, and to accommodate Sir Henry Hoghton of Walton Hall the Avenham engine was designed to consume its own smoke, although its tall chimney was over a mile away. In 1817, it was decided to abandon the Penwortham incline in favour of a diversion on an easier gradient that could be worked by horses.

The layout at Walton Summit in 1846.

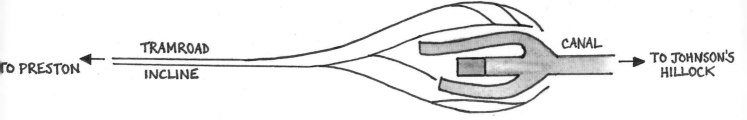

Walton Summit basins, 1968.

Remains of the central warehouse at Walton Summit, 1968.

Weighbridge house at the foot of Walton Summit incline, 1971.

A 9ft tram rail found near Walton-le-Dale, probably removed from Avenham incline, Preston, 1971.

Stone sleeper blocks on the site of the tramroad near Todd Lane, Bamber Bridge, 1971.

**Tramroad
embankment near**
Todd Lane, 1971.

The top of
Penwortham incline
through the gate at
Carr Wood, with the
1817 diversion to the
left.

**Penwortham
embankment, looking**
south, 1971.

The first train

The *Blackburn Mail* recorded the first train in June 1803:

'on the first instant, a Boat laden with coal was navigated on the Lancaster Canal thro' the tunnel at Whittle Hills, and her cargo was discharged into waggons at the termination of the canal at Walton. Twenty-seven waggons were laden, each containing about one ton, and were drawn by one horse, a mile and a half, along the rail road, to the works of Messrs. Claytons, at Bamber Bridge. The waggons extended one hundred yards in length along the railroad, Geo Clayton of Lostock Hall Esq., rode upon the first waggon and the tops of the others were fully occupied. The intention of navigating a boat through the Tunnel, upon this day, was not generally known; it was quickly circulated; old and young left their habitations and employments to witness a sight so novel, and before the Boat reached her discharging place, she was completely crowded with passengers [presumably sitting on the coal] who anxiously rushed into her at every bridge. The workmen were regaled with ale at Bamber Bridge; and among the toasts of the party were given, "The glorious First of June", "The Memory of Lord Howe", and "The healths of those surviving that memorable day".'

The number of wagons obviously was an exaggeration because the maximum permitted was four 'larger' wagons carrying two tons or six 'smaller', evidently a change in Cartwright's original proposal. In any case, even if trains were divided at the inclines the maximum within the capacity of one horse on level track would be no more than about six. The tramroad onward to Preston was finished northbound in November and southbound in January next year, but Cartwright only just lived long enough to see it, dying on 19 January 1804, probably from overwork.

Some wagons were provided by the canal company; others by individual traders, which had to be marked with a letter and number, of which the company kept a register. Through traffic in coal was carried at 1½d per ton/mile on the South End, a flat rate of 1s per ton on the tramroad, and 1d per ton/mile on the North End. Rates for general goods on the tramroad but not using the canal were 4d per ton/mile from Walton to Bamber Bridge, 6d to Todd Lane, 8d to the foot of Penwortham incline and 1s to Preston. Bye-laws for use were introduced progressively as experience dictated, including a limit of 1¼ tons per wagon after heavier loads broke tramplates. In 1828, a new bye-law prohibited drivers from 'sleeping in a waggon or otherwise not attending to his load'. Wagons were hitched to the chains equidistantly, the Avenham chain being able to take six at a time. Breakages were not infrequent, causing wagons to run back down an incline with consequent injuries and sometimes death to men and horses. It appears from later accounts that coal, limestone and other minerals were carried over the tramroad in iron boxes, thus facilitating easy transhipment to and from barges at each end; no doubt an idea picked up by Cartwright when he visited the Peak Forest Canal tramroad, where lower tolls were charged if boxes were used.

The opening of the tramroad brought immediate improvement in finances. Toll income in 1803 was £4,853, nearly double in 1804, and in the first half of 1805, £8,241. A first dividend of 0.5 per cent was declared in 1803, then 1 per cent in 1805, at which rate it stood for nearly 20 years. By 1811 total revenue had nearly tripled, at £15,550.

Since 1794, William Miller of Preston had acted as Cartwright's assistant; he now assumed Cartwright's responsibilities. Cartwright had been an ingenious engineer, including improving the canal's water supply. He produced a scheme to take water from the River Keer at Rennie's aqueduct at Capernwray, south of Tewitfield, suggesting a series of

The Old Tram Bridge, Preston, c1863, showing the wheel at the foot of Avenham incline.

The Old Tram Bridge as rebuilt in reinforced concrete, photographed in 1953.

The Old Tram Bridge looking along the deck, with Avenham incline beyond, 1953.

An oil painting by Thomas Lynch, 'View of Avenham Park' c1862, showing the Old Tram Bridge. (*courtesy Harris Museum, Preston*)

reservoirs upstream on Docker Moor. They would feed the canal via the river and a pump at Capernwray, operated by an existing waterwheel at the mill alongside and below the canal. Riparian owners and the mill proprietors objected, so the scheme appears to have been abandoned in favour of a conventional feeder solely from the river. The east abutment of the aqueduct had a sluice valve and overflow pipe where excess water could be let out into the river at times of high water, now replaced by a concrete spillway. Cartwright also designed and supervised the making of a tunnel from the Ribble at Preston to the canal, where a 70hp Boulton & Watt steam engine pumped water up from the river through a shaft. Standing in an engine-house on the canal bank opposite Canal Street Mill, it was completed by Miller in 1806. Cartwright also designed a tramroad from Tewitfield to quarries at Kellet Seeds, 1¼ miles long, but it was not built.

CHAPTER 4

COMPLETION TO KENDAL

On a mileage basis, revenue from the South End and the tramroad was proportionately higher than from the North End, showing that much more traffic was centred on Preston than Lancaster, although Lancaster men continued to dominate the committee, while agitation from Westmorland shareholders to complete to Kendal became increasingly vociferous. In 1805, Miller re-surveyed the route north of Tewitfield, proposing two alternatives to Rennie's, although still requiring a 340yd tunnel at Hincaster to serve Wakefields' gunpowder mills at Sedgwick. As an alternative, he suggested a 13 mile long tramroad from Tewitfield, with three inclined planes. The canal scheme he costed at £71,755; the tramroad at £38,575.

At last the Westmorland interests, led by the Wakefields, prevailed and the Hincaster route was approved, ratified by yet another Act in 1807. It authorised variations in Rennie's route to a point north of Hincaster, and tramroads to Farleton Knott, Kellet Seeds and 'within the line of canal', thereby giving retrospective authorisation to the Preston tramroad. Powers were also included to abstract water from Farleton, Stainton and Peasey becks to feed the Kendal level, replacing those in the original Act for taking water from the River Mint.

Peace with the Leeds & Liverpool

In 1810 an accord was at last reached with the Leeds & Liverpool, which had now reached Blackburn from the east

Johnson's Hillock Locks, built by the Lancaster to connect its South End with the Leeds & Liverpool. What became the Walton Summit branch is to the left, 1968.

**Johnson's Hillock
No. 3** lock, 1968.

**Tewitfield locks
before** the M6
motorway was built,
1968.

Stone mile post at Capernwray; 11 miles to Kendal.

Iron ground paddle or sluice gate, Tewitfield locks, 1968.

Tewitfiled Locks after the building of the motorway, 1989.

Tewitfield No. 5 lock and bridge, 1968.

but had no funds to proceed any further. Through traffic to Liverpool was still not possible because of the gap onward to Wigan, so the company swallowed its pride and proposed to the Lancaster that it should use the South End instead of attempting to build its own parallel route. The Lancaster seized the opportunity to gain extra revenue and the result was an agreement that the Leeds & Liverpool would extend from Blackburn to Wheelton, near Chorley, ½ mile from the South End, to which the Lancaster would build seven locks up from Johnson's Hillock to meet it, rising 64ft. The Lancaster would also make a ½ mile connection from its termination above Wigan to the top of a series of locks to be built by the Leeds & Liverpool down to the canalised Douglas Navigation. All this work was completed in 1816, when the Leeds & Liverpool at last was officially opened throughout on 19 October and the Lancaster committee joined in a celebratory lunch at Johnson's Hillock.

Management criticism

Despite having bought 56 acres of land for a reservoir at Killington, between Kendal and Sedbergh, to feed the canal, the committee had still made no moves to complete it, despite more growing disquiet from Westmorland shareholders. In 1811, the committee's competence was challenged by a group of Liverpool shareholders, accusing it of favouritism in placing contracts, particularly several members who, with Gregson, were charged with promoting their own trading and colliery interests. A committee of investigation decided that the charges were unfounded, instead praising Gregson and his associates for risking their capital by setting up as carriers in 1797 to promote trade on the canal, to the company's ultimate benefit. Gregson was complimented on his efforts, which were many and varied, often exceeding his official duties, acting alongside the engineer as what today would be the canal's general manager:

'To his enterprise on the opening of the Canal, and to his subsequent indefatigable exertion, united with those of the Committee, may be attributed the progressive increase in the Tonnage Duties.'
The committee was also complimented for raising capital on their own securities when no more demands from shareholders could be made.

However, the criticism of the committee had some effect as moves were now made to complete the canal to Kendal. In 1812, Thomas Fletcher was appointed engineer. He was from a family of engineers and had previously worked for the company as Eastburn's assistant in charge of earthworks on the South End. His first job was to prepare detailed estimates, producing a figure of £98,095 and an anticipated revenue of £7,589 a year. Accordingly, work was authorised in 1813. Even then several Preston shareholders insisted that it was more important to replace the tramroad with canal, suggesting that the Ribble could be crossed on the level. Fletcher dismissed the idea as impracticable, as he did another proposal for a low-level aqueduct approached by locks, costing £160,537. But the dissidents persisted, maintaining that it could be financed by a loan from the Exchequer Bill Loan Commissioners and demanding a special general meeting in 1817, thereby creating even more delay. The committee refused.

Northward from Tewitfield

Meanwhile work had begun on the three biggest jobs: the eight locks at Tewitfield, rising 75ft; the 378 yd. long Hincaster tunnel; and Killington reservoir. The last entailed building a dam across the valley of Peasey Beck, which would be used to convey the waters to the canal at Crooklands. In May 1817, William Crosley Jr. was appointed engineer in charge of the works. He was the son of the William Crosley who had worked under Rennie and had been his assistant in surveying the Rochdale Canal, later becoming its engineer.

New Mill Aqueduct,
Holme, 1987.

**Burton Road
Aqueduct,** Holme,
1987.

Holme bridges; looking north through Janson's Bridge to Warehouse and Holme Park bridges. The larch tree plantations are typical on the Northern Reaches, 1971.

Duke's Bridge, Farleton, showing the 'cattle creep' on the right, 1971.

The canal in the landscape: looking north from Farleton Knott, 1968. The broad scar in the middle distance is the M6 motorway under construction.

Crooklands Aqueduct over Stainton Beck, 1989.

Killington reservoir, 1969.

The feeder from Killington at Crooklands, 1989.

The east end of Hincaster Tunnel, showing on the left the horsepath tunnel under the railway, 1988.

An accommodation bridge crossing Hincaster Tunnel horsepath, 1991.

An old photograph of the west end of Hincaster Tunnel, showing fishing, pleasure boating. (*courtesy Kendal Library*)

The same view in 1968.

An iron stanchion for the hauling chain in Hincaster Tunnel, 2009.

Sedgwick Aqueduct, 1975.

On the Lancaster he relieved Fletcher of the added responsibility of the new work, and on Christmas Day the tunnel was completed. Fletcher had advocated lining it with brick to save money, but the committee was doubtful. Brick to them was an alien material. To allay their misgivings several members and Gregson embarked on a tour of canals in the Midlands to inspect tunnels lined with brick, and as a result they compromised and agreed to a brick lining at Hincaster, but only above the water line, insisting on stone beneath. Suitable brick-making clay was found not far away in a field west of Heversham, where a small brickworks was set up and made some two million bricks.

By November 1818 the locks were ready and Killington reservoir was filling, reaching a capacity of 700 million gallons. The rest of the canal was completed early in 1819, twenty-two years after the opening of the first section. The first cargo to Kendal was delayed while a burst in the embankment at Crooklands was repaired, but on 14 April a barge-load of paving stones from Farleton was delivered.

To Kendal at last

The official opening took place on 18 June when John Pearson, mayor of Kendal, the corporation and Kendal shareholders walked in procession from the mayor's house to Aynham Wharf, preceded by 'Constables and other Officers' to the accompaniment of a band and gunfire from cannon on Castle Hill. There they embarked on the *City Barge* and, accompanied by boats decorated with flags, set off southward at 10a.m.

It seems to have been a somewhat subdued event at first. The following day's *Westmorland Advertiser and Kendal Chronicle* reported:

'... *a most feeble and heart-depressing shout was raised – some four caps were lifted from the head, but the surrounding multitudes preserved an obstinate and most provoking silence, though twice invited to lend their assistance to the cheer. The voyage commenced under these auspices, but as the barge is understood to have been well-provisioned, we hope the fair ladies and gallant crew will suffer no other disappointments from the voyage.*'

No doubt fortified by the liquid provisions as the day went on, matters steadily improved. At Crooklands the mayoral party met two north-bound boats that had left Lancaster at 7a.m. carrying the canal company committee, officials and principal shareholders. Together they returned to Kendal, arriving at 4.15p.m. where 'an immense multitude, lining the banks of the Canal, and assembled on the Castle Hill, greeted their safe arrival in port'. A more detailed account appeared in the following week's edition. It was a day 'long memorable amongst the inhabitants of Kendal,' beginning with a specially composed poem of fifteen verses. Sixteen boats returned from Crooklands, three carrying bands, and including five fly-boats 'plentifully furnished with provisions, wine and other liquers [sic]'. Crowds lined the banks and bridges, and more guns were fired from both sides of the town. After disembarking the party formed a procession to the Town Hall where 116 ticket-holders at 15s (75p) each sat down to dinner, presided over by the mayor. It was advertised to take place at 4pm, so evidently was rather late.

One of the eighteen toasts was to Samuel Gregson who, in his reply, included a somewhat wry reference to the enquiry of 1811. Talking about his 27 years' service, it was reported that he commented that it had been '... next to impossible to give satisfaction to all parties,' that he had to combat 'the prejudices of a great many, and it was possible that the interests of a great many might be injured, but the approbation of so numerous and respectable a company, interested in the concern, was to him a high recommendation.' In the evening, a ball

'On the Canal, Kendal', from an old photograph. (*courtesy Kendal Library*)

Kendal Change Bridge, The Lound, from an old photograph. (*courtesy Kendal Library*)

Canal Head, Kendal, from the castle, c1880-90. The building on the bottom right hand corner of the basin was the former Packet Boat House, (*courtesy Kendal Library*)

Unloading coal at Canal Head. (*courtesy Margaret Duff Collection, Kendal*)

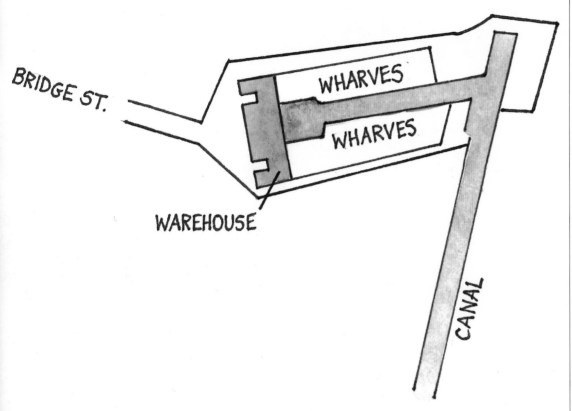

Canal Head, Kendal, 1819.

for 100 people was held at the King's Arms, Kendal, lasting from 9pm to 3 o'clock the next morning. At the same time two more public dinners were held for 'fifty gentlemen at each.'

On 3 September, another burst in the bank closed the canal for a week. After the embankment at Killington was raised several times, by September 1820 the reservoir finally covered 153 acres and was 53ft deep. Shortly afterwards a leak was discovered near the foot of the dam and the reservoir had to be drained while it was repaired.

CHAPTER 5

THE CANAL AT WORK

The last chapter touched on the immediate effect of the canal's opening to Preston and Lancaster. Preston's cotton-spinning industry was already growing, at first using water power, then steam for which the coal came either by road, down the Douglas or around the coast to the Ribble. After the opening of the South End of the canal and the tramroad, expansion grew rapidly. In the fifty years after 1801 the population grew six-fold, helped after 1838 by the railway.

The opening of the canal to Kendal was seized on by the Lancaster shareholders to press for the branch canal to Glasson Dock, already authorised in the 1792

Act. They saw it as a means of no longer relying on the Lune to sustain Lancaster as a port, and proposed seeking a further Act to raise more capital. Preston, however, considered that crossing the Ribble and eliminating the tramroad should have priority as a means of further reducing the price of coal, claiming that money had already been wasted in 'ornamenting' the town of Lancaster with a grand aqueduct over the Lune, upon which 'the water has lain stagnant for over twenty years.' However, the Lancaster men got their way and in 1819 an Act was secured to raise £270,000 by mortgaging the tolls to finance the branch and repay debts, at the same

Looking north to Hest Bank Bridge, 1962.

time retrospectively authorising Killington reservoir and the Leeds & Liverpool connection at Johnson's Hillock.

Simultaneously, consideration was given to making a short connection to the sea at Hest Bank on Morecambe Bay, where the canal was only ¼ mile from the shore. Instead, in 1820 a Kendal & Hest Bank Shipping Company built a stone pier and breakwater for transhipping goods to and from Kendal. Crosley estimated the cost, with a dock (not built), at £69,591. There was regular trade with Liverpool twice a week, also serving places north by road, such as Penrith, Hawes and Kirkby Stephen. The canal company offered shippers using Hest Bank a discount of 1s 8d (8½p) per ton on merchandise traffic to Kendal.

The Glasson branch
In 1820, Crosley was appointed superintendent of the whole canal,

and he estimated the cost of a Glasson branch to be £34,608. If it was made, the Lancaster Port Commissioners, within whose jurisdiction Glasson fell, agreed to drastically reduce their port charges from 1s 3d (6p) per ton to 4d (1.7p), hoping that the branch canal would take import and export trade away from Preston. The canal company, for its part, undertook to pay the Port Commissioners £500 and a guaranteed annual income of £200 from charges for direct shipping between Glasson and Ireland, the Isle of Man, and ports beyond Holyhead and Galloway.

Consequently, it was decided to press ahead with the Glasson branch, and by December 1825 it was ready; 2½ miles, from the canal at Galgate down six locks falling 52ft to a large basin fed by the River Conder and capable of taking 200 ton vessels, followed by a further lock into the dock and thence by a sea-lock into the Lune estuary. The basin was used for

The entrance to the Glasson Dock branch and top lock, Galgate, 1959.

Thurnham Mill and lock, 1968.

The Glasson branch drained for repairs below Lock 2, 1985.

The end of the Glasson branch looking towards the freshwater basin, 1969.

The freshwater basin at Glasson, with the canal entrance at the far side, 1969.

Glasson Dock, 1969.

SHIPPING, GLASSON DOCK, NEAR LANCASTER.

E8094.

Glasson Dock was used for taking delivery of coal imported during the 1983 miners' strike.

Glasson Dock in the 1930s, from an old postcard.

Glasson Dock warehouse, demolished in 1940. (*courtesy Lancaster City Museum*)

scouring out the dock and as a reservoir for it at low tides. Trade was slow at first, until money was available to build wharves and a five-storey warehouse. Water was abstracted from the River Conder above Thurnham Mill, situated alongside the lowest lock, which the canal purchased for £1,000 in 1824 in order to secure its water rights. Sufficient water was let out from the canal to drive the mill wheel, returning to the canal below it, which in turn now fed the freshwater basin at Glasson. In 1836, a small shipyard was opened at the dock, its first vessel being a 70ft canal barge *Acorn*. The dry dock in which it was built was filled in around 1980 after having been disused since 1968.

Economic effects

While the new branch did something to improve trade at the Port of Lancaster, the benefit to Preston was the greater. In 1803, the Ribble Navigation Company was incorporated to improve the river up to the town, but was largely ineffective until 1834, when a scheme was promoted to cut a nine-mile ship canal from Lytham, which Fletcher surveyed and costed at £101,078. The proposal failed from lack of support, but in 1838 a new Ribble Navigation Company cut a new channel in the estuary to wharves it built at Preston. That, too, failed, largely because a dock was opened at Lytham in 1842. Yet a third Ribble Company was formed in 1853, equally unsuccessfully, until Preston Corporation bought it and built Preston Dock, opened in 1892 and capable of taking ocean-going vessels. The failure of the successive navigation companies was mainly due to the constantly shifting channels in the estuary, but also to a large extent to the ability of the Lancaster Canal to take coastal craft carrying 60 tons or more to Preston from Glasson. In 1829 the Ribble Company complained that ships from Scotland and Ireland were reaching Preston direct via Glasson, with no need to tranship into lighters off Lytham, saving 1s 1d (5p) on a ton of merchandise. In 1840, 185 ships entered the canal at Glasson, carrying 12,128 tons, sailing from ports as far as Ireland, the Isle of Man, Holyhead and Galloway, while only 62 berthed at Lancaster quay on the Lune.

But the greatest beneficiary of Glasson, proportionately, was Kendal. Hitherto, trade was reliant on pack horses or wagons on often poorly-maintained turnpike roads, and coastal shipping to Milnthorpe subject to the tides of

Morecambe Bay and the River Kent. The opening of the canal transformed the town. A population of 2,500 in 1730 grew over five times, to 7,500 by 1811 and 12,000 by 1851. Kendal Corporation asked the canal company to extend its proposed terminus a short distance to the end of Miller Bridge over the Kent, in return undertaking to build a basin, wharves and a large warehouse. They rebuilt Miller Bridge to improve access from the town, begun in 1818 in anticipation of the arrival of the canal. It cost the corporation £7,000, set against an annual income of some £550 a year from rents and wharfage charges. A special Kendal canal committee was formed to oversee the work. The Corporation's basin was set at a slightly acute angle from the end of the canal, with two arms leading into the warehouse. In a town previously noted mainly for woollen cloth, new industrial development followed rapidly, extending along the canal itself for ½ mile to a gas works and later, in the 1880s, an electricity works, both reliant on the canal for coal. Across the river the town itself improved immensely. In 1861, Cornelius Nicholson wrote in *The Annals of Kendal*:

'In a very short time, the town assumed a new and modern appearance – so very different that any person having been absent for a few years, could scarcely have identified it'.

As well as Preston, Lancaster and Kendal, the canal benefited other, smaller communities along its length. At Knowley Wharf (later known as Botany Wharf) it passed ½ mile from Chorley, a centre for coal mining and quarrying, where a population of 4,500 in 1801 had doubled by 1824. It brought impetus to the small town of Garstang's trade through a large basin close by. To Kirkham, though, it was less useful. As noted in Chapter 2, the nearest wharf was at Salwick, three miles away. The town's cloth trade relied largely on a long-established wharf and warehouse on the Wyre, five miles away. In 1824, Edward Baines in his *History, Directory and Gazetteer of the County Palatine of Lancaster* commented that, '… it has long been a matter of regret that a collateral branch has not yet been cut to complete the communication of Kirkham', although a branch canal had been considered several times. On the other hand, the branch canal from Glasson enabled small coastal craft to sail up to Kendal, bringing about the rapid decline of Milnthorpe as a port. Sandside continued to receive some shipping until the building of Arnside railway viaduct cut it off in 1857.

The barge *Pet* unloading coal next to Penny St. Bridge, Lancaster, before the bridge was rebuilt in 1899-1900. (*courtesy Lancaster City Museum*)

The maintenance yard at Lancaster, 1969.

Former boat horse stables, Lancaster, 1969.

Looking north from Penny Street Bridge, Lancaster, 2009.

Another view of Canal Head, Kendal, from the castle, c1880-90. (*courtesy Kendal Library*)

A boat load of coal passing through Lea Lane Bridge, Salwick, in 1910. The piles of hay were to feed the horses en route.

Kirkham Road Bridge, near Catforth, known as 'Hand and Dagger Bridge' after the adjacent pub, 2008.

Former stables at Swillbrook Wharf, Catforth, 1971.

Garstang Basin, 1969, showing original warehouse.

Trading on the canal

Once the Glasson branch had been completed, Crosley resigned in 1826 in order to become engineer to the Macclesfield Canal. Gregson's second son, Bryan Padgett Gregson, took over as engineer and superintendent. He had assisted his father since about 1813, an able administrator, who for some years had been in charge of the general management of the canal and had been prominent in developing swift packet boat or 'fly-boat' services carrying small consignments and parcels. Chorley, for instance, had daily fly-boats to Blackburn, Manchester, Liverpool and Leeds from Knowley wharf, via the Leeds & Liverpool and other canals. Even a small place like Carnforth, which in 1821 had only 294 inhabitants but served as an access point for a large area of north Lancashire and south Westmorland, enjoyed daily packet services to Lancaster and Kendal, which themselves had twice-daily fly-boats. They carried passengers in fore and aft cabins, roughly equivalent to present-day first and second class respectively. Some sailings were overnight. In 1825 the fares from Preston to Lancaster and Lancaster to Kendal were three shillings (about 15p) in the fore cabin, and two shillings in the aft-cabin. Intermediate journeys between Preston, Garstang, Lancaster and Kendal were charged at 1½ old pence (say 0.75p) per mile. Trade through Glasson continued to grow. In 1831 the Hest Bank Company moved its operations to Glasson and Hest Bank ceased to be a port.

The maximum size of craft on the canal was 72ft long and 14ft 3in beam, with a draught of 3ft 10in, loading to 48-50 tons. Mersey flats, the flat-bottomed sailing barges which operated around the coast to Glasson, were up to 70ft long x 14ft 3in beam, with a shallow draught of only 1ft 10in making them capable of loading up to 80 tons. On the South End, the principal craft were 62ft long Leeds & Liverpool short-boats. All craft were horse-drawn, usually by two, for which stables and fodder stores were provided along the canal. Coastal vessels coming on to the canal could use their sails to assist where possible, although the frequency of bridges, requiring masts to be unstepped, generally made it impracticable. Boats had a crew of two, a man and a boy, who slept on board. In later years when railway competition forced economies, families living on board formed the crew. On the South End, Leeds & Liverpool steamers later became common, usually towing one or two dumb barges, but on the North End, horse-operation continued.

Looking at the canal company's economic progress up to 1823, we find that £600,000 had been spent on capital works, not including the Glasson branch, while in that year gross income was £28,874 compared with £16,715 thirteen years earlier. The principal bulk traffic northward was coal, and new pits were opened close to the South End. Southward it was slate and limestone from north Lancashire and Westmorland, for which kilns were set up close to the canal to burn it into lime. There were banks of limekilns at sundry places on both ends of the canal; the 1847 6in Ordnance Survey map shows over twenty alongside or close to the North End, and two on the South End, together with numbers of quarries, gravel pits, brick and tile works, several malt kilns and, on the South End in particular, cotton and flax mills, bleach and print works. Collieries predominated between Wigan and Chorley, many with connecting tramroads or railways. There was also a colliery at Farleton, on the North End, which was worked intermittently from the late sixteenth century until at least 1847. A connecting tramroad from Farleton Knott quarries, north of Tewitfield, to the canal empowered in the 1807 Act was not proceeded with. The wharf, warehouse and access road still standing at Farleton were doubtless constructed for the lime trade. A short branch was built into a large limestone quarry at Capernwray, south of the locks. There was also a number of 'cinder ovens' for burning coal into coke for various ironworks and foundries, including at Kendal, Carnforth and Preston.

Haymaking on the towing path near Galgate, 1947.

Barge *Iron Duke* (Baines of Preston) near Holme Park Quarry 1907.

Remains of lime kiln next to Tulketh Aqueduct, Preston, 1971.

The canal opposite the Packet Boat Hotel, Bolton-le-Sands, from an old postcard.

BLS.30F   CANAL & PACKET BOAT HOTEL, BOLTON-LE-SANDS

COPYRIGHT FRITH LTD

The canal at Farleton; old warehouse on the right, 1989.

Farleton warehouse from the rear, 2008.

New England Cottages and canal arm to quarry, Capernwray, 1968.

The same view after demolition of the cottages, 1989.

After the tramroad was completed coal trading from Wigan to Preston became increasingly competitive. There was now a second route added to the existing one down the Leeds & Liverpool's Douglas Navigation to the Ribble and thence to Preston up the estuary or via Freckleton Creek. After the Glasson branch was opened in 1825 a third was available. Both the traders and the two canal companies frequently adjusted their charges and tolls, until the coming of the railways after 1840 effectively ended coal traffic solely bound for Preston.

Canal carriers
There were two main carriers on the canal, the Wigan Coal and Iron Company and John Hargreaves & Son, also of Wigan.

The Hargreaves family had been in the carrying business for generations; road, then canal and finally on several Lancashire railways, including the Lancaster & Preston Junction line. They occupied a powerful position in the carrying trade. There were also smaller carriers, such as William Welsh, who like Hargreaves, operated packet boats. Another was John Brockbank of Lancaster, a canal committeeman and boat builder who also made lock gates, bridge centring, wheelbarrows and other timber-work for building the canal. His father, George, built his first ship in 1763 and later opened a yard at Glasson. Others went on to repair canal boats there: sixty-seven belonging to eleven different owners were worked on between 1841 and 1930, when canal work ceased.

Crane on stone loading pier at the end of the former tramroad from New England quarry, 1989.

J & S Baines' barge *Joseph* near Garstang, 1907.

A laden coal barge proceeding northward near Hest Bank, 1934.

Dan and Mary
Ashcroft aboard their
barge, c1934.

Empty barges at Preston basin during the 1921 coal strike.

Barges undergoing repairs at Preston, c1920.

Baling out at Preston, c1920.

A maintenance boat at the Wyre Aqueduct, Garstang, from an old picture postcard, 1920s.

The Wigan Coal & Iron Company's boat *Express* at one of the wooden lift bridges, Preston basin, c. 1920.

Some larger canals set up their own carrying departments, including the Leeds & Liverpool. The Lancaster did so in a fairly small way, independently of its packet boat services. It was acquired by the London & North Western Railway as part of its purchase in 1885.

All boats were registered in Preston, Lancaster or Kendal. The Wigan company ceased trading in 1928 and their fleet of boats was bought by Baines Brothers of Preston, who in turn stopped trading in 1944, the year of the last traffic to Kendal in October. Most of their boats were broken up. In 1942 a long-established carrying family, the Ashcrofts of Preston, formed Ashcrofts Carriers Ltd with six boats, trading until 1947 when Dan Ashcroft Jr. carried the last load on the canal, coal from Preston to Lancaster.

Final schemes

In 1827, a last scheme to supersede the tramroad was put forward by a Manchester firm of civil engineers, Twyford & Wilson. By this time the Leeds & Liverpool had progressively replaced the Douglas Navigation by a canal from Wigan to Tarleton, leaving just four miles of navigable river to the Ribble estuary opposite Freckleton Creek on the north bank, itself already navigable for a mile to the village. Twyford & Wilson advocated lines of wooden beams across the Ribble, forming a floating towing path, with openings in the middle for navigation channels. They made no mention of how these would be crossed, nor the question of tides. At Freckleton a new canal would be cut eastward to join the North End of the Lancaster near Salwick, rising 79ft 4in by ten locks. A second canal was proposed to run northward past Kirkham and Poulton-le-Fylde to the Wyre estuary at Thornton, close to the point where, twenty years later, the railway port of Fleetwood was built; a total of 11¼ miles of new canal. They costed the scheme at £80,000, but neither the Lancaster nor the Leeds & Liverpool showed any interest.

In the same year the committee suggested that the tramroad could be improved by diverting it on to a longer but easier route at Avenham, thereby avoiding the incline, and widening Fishergate tunnel to take double track. The idea was not followed up, although earlier in 1823 a successful experiment with 9ft long tramplates in the tunnel and on the up-hill line on Avenham incline enabled five coupled wagons to be taken up at a time. In 1828, B.P. Gregson visited two early railways, the Stockton & Darlington Railway and the Bolton & Leigh to observe how they were operated. On his return, he advocated reducing wear and tear on wagons by fitting broader wheels on fixed axles, replacing loose springs, and proper brakes instead of lock chains.

CHAPTER 6

WAR WITH THE RAILWAYS

In 1830, the Liverpool & Manchester Railway was opened, the world's first 'main line' in the modern sense. B.P. Gregson and the committee recognised that railways now threatened to supersede canals instead of being an

The canal and railways around Preston.

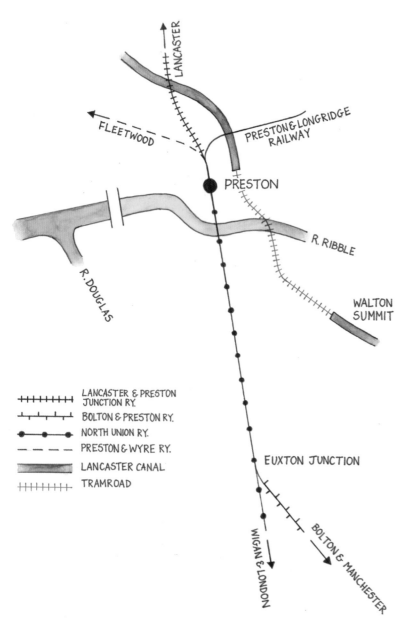

LANCASTER

FLEETWOOD

PRESTON & LONGRIDGE RAILWAY

PRESTON

R. RIBBLE

R. DOUGLAS

WALTON SUMMIT

EUXTON JUNCTION

WIGAN & LONDON

BOLTON & MANCHESTER

+++++++++ LANCASTER & PRESTON JUNCTION RY.

┴─┼─┴─┼─┴ BOLTON & PRESTON RY.

●──●──● NORTH UNION RY.

─ ─ ─ ─ PRESTON & WYRE RY.

▬▬▬▬ LANCASTER CANAL

+++++++++ TRAMROAD

adjunct to them, so he was instructed to economise by reducing staff to the minimum and to estimate the cost of upgrading the tramroad to take locomotives. He produced a figure of £11,650, excluding any necessary diversions and earthworks. Railways were already being projected to Preston from Wigan and from Manchester, the former intending to connect with the Liverpool & Manchester. Gregson advocated that as an alternative, the canal company should collaborate with one of the projected lines by abolishing the tramroad entirely, and dispose of the South End of the canal by offering it to the Leeds & Liverpool which, of course, was already using it. He was far-sighted, going on to express the opinion that even if the current railway schemes were defeated they would be replaced by others. If, however, the committee was determined to oppose the railway from Wigan, the company should project its own line direct from Preston to Liverpool.

The committee then sought advice from George Stephenson on the practicability of converting the tramroad into a railway. After a survey, he suggested it could be done by creating four self-acting inclines between Walton Summit and Penwortham, and an engine-worked incline at Avenham on a new course, estimated at £11,894.15s.0d. (£11,894.75p). Gregson evidently thought little of it; Stephenson was known to advocate inclines to overcome gradients. In Gregson's opinion, the plan would be difficult to execute and, to say the least, operationally inconvenient. At the same time a group of committee members were talking to the promoters of the Wigan & Preston Railway who, in return for the

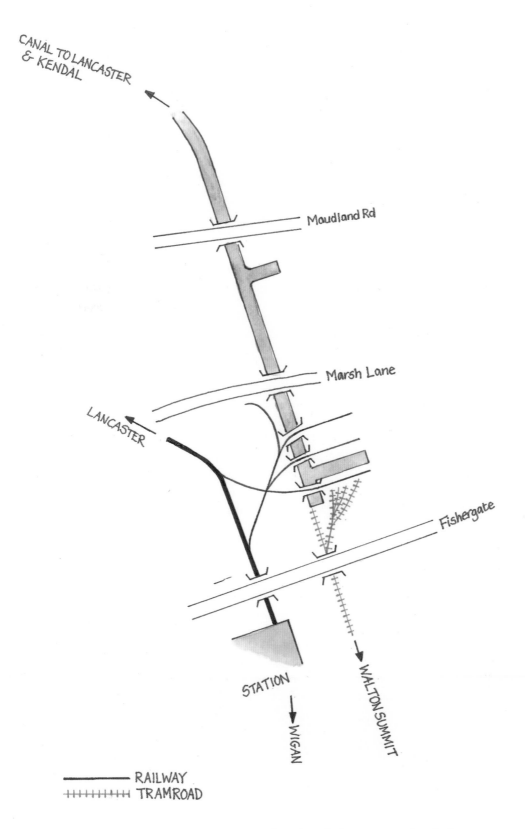

The canal and railway interchange at Preston, 1846.

CANAL TO LANCASTER & KENDAL

Maudland Rd

Marsh Lane

LANCASTER

Fishergate

STATION

WIGAN

WALTON SUMMIT

——— RAILWAY
+++++++++ TRAMROAD

canal company agreeing not to oppose their parliamentary Bill, offered to build a ¼ mile branch from the tramroad at Brownedge to their railway, which would convey cargoes onward to a rail terminus at Preston canal wharf. The full committee dismissed the proposal as being too vague, but the Wigan & Preston carried on and gained Royal Assent to their Bill in April 1831. The canal company simultaneously attempted similar negotiations with the Manchester &

Preston promoters, with no more success, but fortunately gained a temporary reprieve when that railway's Bill failed in parliament.

Disposing of the tramroad

Under Gregson's leadership, the company adopted a policy of competing with railways where they thought they could, and co-operating where it was obvious they could not. The Wigan & Preston project, for example, became part of the larger North Union Railway which aimed to connect with the Liverpool & Manchester at Newton-le-Willows (later to become Earlestown), where it was to be joined by a line from London, now part of the west coast main line to Scotland. It opened in 1833. The North Union was also empowered to build a branch from Wigan to collieries at New Springs, close to the junction with the Leeds & Liverpool at Wigan top lock. It crossed the Lancaster's authorised onward route to Westhoughton, which of course had not been built, but to safeguard its possible future interests the company hastily extended its canal for a few hundred

yards past the top lock, forcing the railway company to build a bridge over it. The canal extension was completely useless, as by this time the Lancaster had given up intentions of continuing on to Westhoughton, but it was part of a game of tit-for-tat following the North Union's refusal to include in its Bill clauses protecting the canal. It also made the North Union realise that it could not ride roughshod over a rival concern.

In the previous year the canal had taken the opposite stance over the Bolton & Preston Railway Bill. The railway wanted to take over the tramroad and use its course for a route into Preston, offering to take a lease in perpetuity, together with some canal company land for a station near the Preston canal basin, all at a suggested rent of £8,000 per year, together with a short siding to the basin enabling an exchange of traffic, and a locomotive reserved solely for hauling trains of canal traffic that hitherto had been carried along the tramroad. The proposed lease would include tolls from the Lancaster's traffic on the South End of the canal, but not the Leeds & Liverpool's. In return, the

Site of tramroad between Bamber Bridge and Brownedge, 1953. The bridge under the railway at Bamber Bridge Junction was altered in 1850, creating the bend in the tramroad site.

Looking south from Moss Bridge towards Whittle Hills tunnels on the South End, 1968.

canal company would undertake not to oppose the railway's Bill in parliament. Full agreement was reached in January 1837, and the Bolton & Preston gained its Act in July. Then, seeing that the North Union's Bill seemed likely to succeed, the Bolton Company changed its mind about using the tramroad route and instead in 1838 obtained a further Act empowering it to gain access to Preston over the North Union from a junction at Euxton, some six miles to the south at Leyland. Now, of course, it found itself encumbered with the tramroad, for which it had no use, but which the canal company did not want back. After amalgamating with the Bolton & Preston in 1844, the North Union agreed to maintain it for canal traffic at a reduced annual rental of £7,400, later reduced by the Lancaster to £7,000 rather than agree to granting preferential rates for coal traffic transhipped from the railway at Preston.

It was a smart move by Gregson and the committee. Gregson foresaw that the railway would gradually erode the canal's coal trade as branch railways were built to neighbouring collieries, and he pressed the committee to concentrate on traffic coming on to the canal from the railway at Preston, bound for established industries served by the North End. As he anticipated, tramroad traffic began to decline, showing that the company had done the right thing in disposing of it when the chance came. In 1839, tolls on the South End and the tramroad brought in £10,000 to the Bolton & Preston, but only £1,000 net profit after paying for maintenance and repairs.

By 1850, the North Union was losing £5,000 a year on the tramroad which, under the terms of the lease, it had to keep open. Gregson had been proved right.

Swift passenger boats

While making these moves the Lancaster strengthened its position north of Preston. The committee had long seen that eventually a railway would be projected northward, so in 1832 it had sought to forestall potential competition by introducing a swift passenger service on the canal. Gregson and a party from the committee visited the Glasgow Paisley & Ardrossan Canal to sample that company's swift passenger boats. They were lightly built to narrow dimensions, with a shallow draught and a pointed bow, enabling them to sit lightly on the water. On the party's return one was ordered, named *Waterwitch*, and on 1 April 1833 it began a daily service between Preston and Lancaster, extended to Kendal on alternate days, and returning on the next day. A second craft, *Swiftsure*, was delivered in the following year. They were joined by a third boat, *Swallow*, in August 1835. The voyage from Preston to Kendal took eight hours, compared with ten with the old packet boats, and the new boats were drawn at a swift trot by two horses at a speed of ten miles an hour. Horses were changed every five miles and stables were built at eleven changing points. Boat houses and ticket offices were built at Preston, Lancaster and Kendal, together with a 'passenger waiting shed' at Preston; in short, all the appurtenances of a railway station. A further swift boat began sailing in May 1839. It was named *Crewdson*, after the chairman William Dilworth Crewdson. It enabled a thrice-daily service to Kendal. Stops were made at Salwick, Garstang, Potters Brook (bridge 81, for Forton), Galgate, Lancaster, Hest Bank, Bolton-le-Sands, Carnforth, Capernwray (for Borwick), Tewitfield (where passengers walked up the locks to a waiting second boat), Burton, Farleton, Crooklands, Hincaster and Sedgwick. Each boat could carry up to 100 passengers and had two cabins, heated in the winter, and refreshments were served on board. After 1838, sailings from Preston were timed to meet trains from the south and a horse-bus took passengers to the canal basin; later repeated at Lancaster for passengers to Kendal. The entire operation was smoothly efficient. Indeed, it had to be in order to compete with the coming railway, the Lancaster & Preston Junction company, opened in 1840, to which the canal sold some land for a station at Preston. There was now a continuous rail route from London to Lancaster.

In 1836, it was realised that Killington reservoir and feeders north of Tewitfield provided enough water, so the Ribble pumping engine was sold. On the South End, following three collapses, 150yd of Whittle Hills tunnel was opened out to form two separate short tunnels. The Glasson branch was becoming increasingly profitable. That year was the best in the canal's existence, bringing in revenue of £34,200 and enabling a dividend of £1.7s (£1.34p) to be declared. At this time, there was talk about connecting Preston basin to the proposed Preston & Lytham Ship Canal; they would have been only 600yd apart, but no more was heard of it, any more than similar schemes earlier. In 1841 the dividend reached £1.10s (£1.50p).

But all was not well in the developing railway world. The Bolton & Preston, North Union and Lancaster & Preston companies were squabbling over Preston stations. Yet another company, the

Preston & Wyre to Fleetwood, opened in July 1840, offered a service to Scotland via steamers from Fleetwood to Ardrossan. When the Lancaster & Preston opened a month earlier in 1840 it offered a cut-price rail-and-road fare of 4s (20p) from Preston to Kendal, to which the canal company responded by halving its fare. By offering not only a cheaper fare but a much smoother and more comfortable through journey, the canal lost no passengers.

Running a railway

The Lancaster & Preston, which had an agreement to work its own trains over the Bolton & Preston, was now in severe financial difficulty, so it sought to be taken over by the North Union or the Bolton & Preston, but those companies had enough problems of their own and showed no interest. Again, the canal company seized an opportunity and offered to take over the railway on a 21-years lease at £13,500 a year, which on 1 September 1842 the Lancaster & Preston was only too glad to accept. The lease was retrospectively

The swift passenger boat *Waterwitch* in use as an engineers' inspection boat, seen here alongside the packet boat house at Lancaster. (*courtesy Lancaster Museum*)

A handbill and timetable for the swift passenger boat service, 1833.

Canal Packet Boats.

BETWEEN

Kendal, Lancaster, & Preston.

THE NEW

SWIFT BOAT,

CALLED

" The WATER WITCH"

WILL be employed between LANCASTER and PRESTON,
for the present, and perform the distance of
30 Miles in about three hours.

THE BOATS WILL SAIL

On MONDAY the 1st April,

From *Kendal* to *Preston*, and from *Preston* to
Kendal, on alternate days, (Sundays excepted.)

The Packet will leave KENDAL at SIX o'Clock in the Morning, andn
LANCASTER at ONE o'Clock, every *MONDAY*, *WEDNESDAY*,
and *FRIDAY*, and arrive at PRESTON soon after FOUR o'Clock,

And will leave PRESTON *at half after* NINE o'Clock, and LANCASTER at
ONE o'Clock, every *TUESDAY*, *THURSDAY*, and *SATURDAY*,
and arrive at KENDAL, at half-past SEVEN o'Clock.

FARES.

FIRST CABIN.—The whole length — — — — — Six Shillings;
Between *Kendal* and *Lancaster*,}
   or *Lancaster* and *Preston*,} Three Shillings;
shorter distances, *three half-pence* per Mile;
but no Fare less than Nine Pence.

SECOND CABIN.—The whole length — — — — Four Shillings;
Between *Kendal* and *Lancaster*,}
   or *Lancaster* and *Preston*,} Two Shillings;
shorter distances, *one penny* per Mile;
but no Fare less than Six Pence.

☞ *The Boat will sail from Kendal an hour earlier than heretofore, and
both boats will leave Lancaster at ONE o'clock.*

*** Small Parcels between *Lancaster* and *Preston*, or *Lancaster* and
Kendal, Six Pence each, the whole length between *Preston* and *Kendal*,
One Shilling each, delivered free of Porterage,

Lancaster, March 28th, 1833.

The packet boat house at Lancaster, 1996. It has now been restored and converted into flats.

The opened-out section of Whittle Hills tunnel while it still held water, 1953.

authorised by a Lancaster & Preston Act of 1843, the same year in which two lines from Lancaster to Carlisle were projected. One took a route up the Lune Valley and the other through Kendal. The canal company supported the Lune proposal because it did not represent direct competition, even offering to invest £50,000, but was compelled to withdraw it in order to obtain support for the Lancaster & Preston lease.

There was now the unprecedented situation of a canal company taking over a railway in order to eliminate competition when the opposite was the norm elsewhere. The Lancaster proceeded to effectively 'milk' the railway, beginning by withdrawing the Preston to Lancaster passenger boats, increasing the railway fares and removing seats from the third-class carriages so that more passengers could be carried standing. Goods traffic was in the hands of the carriers, Hargreaves & Son, who also acted for other railways in the north-west. The canal company now took it into its own hands, thereby creating a local transport monopoly: passengers and merchandise by rail; coal and minerals by canal. The canal fully exploited its position, making a profit of £5,000 from the railway in the first year, increasing in each successive year. As the lease included the use of the railway company's locomotives, the canal company undertook to work the Manchester Bolton & Bury Railway's onward traffic from Bolton to Preston in conjunction with its own as lessee of the Lancaster & Preston, thereby competing with the North Union for Manchester-Preston traffic.

The question of the routes from Lancaster northward was resolved by the promotion of the Lancaster & Carlisle Railway, running via Kendal and thus directly competing with the canal. The Lancaster promptly offered to operate the North End of the canal and the Glasson branch 'for and on behalf of the railway' in return for a guaranteed annual income of £11,000, with effect from 1 January 1846.

Evidently it foresaw a dramatic fall in income once the Lancaster & Carlisle was opened, and the arrangement was provisionally agreed. The canal also offered the Lancaster & Carlisle the unexpired portion of its lease of the Lancaster & Preston Junction line for £1,250 a year, together with stone from its Lancaster quarry for construction work. Further, it wanted the railway to take over its wharves at Preston as part of the lease, but the parties failed to agree, so in what appears to have been a fit of pique the canal company cut off negotiations and formally opposed the Lancaster & Carlisle Bill in parliament. The strategy failed, and the railway got its Act in June 1844.

Doubtless preoccupied by these manoeuvres, it was October 1843 before the canal presented a formal draft lease to the Lancaster & Preston Junction board, thirteen months after the authorising Act. In that time, the Lancaster & Preston Junction had been having second thoughts about leasing itself to the canal. The draft included clauses permitting the canal to sub-lease the railway, probably seen as an escape route when the Lancaster & Carlisle was opened. The leasing Act was couched only in general terms, so a sub-lease would have been in order. Consequently, the Lancaster & Preston Junction objected, probably to buy time while it tried to lease itself to the Lancaster & Carlisle, which it did in October 1844; something which, in the absence of a formal lease to the canal company, it was quite at liberty to do. While all this had been going on another player appeared on the stage; a proposed east-west railway from Skipton to Lancaster and what later became Morecambe, the North Western Railway – known later as the 'Little' North Western to avoid confusion with the much larger London & North Western. The canal company had co-operated by allowing the proposed new line to pass beneath one of the arches of the Lune aqueduct, but the Lancaster & Preston Junction board viewed it as a potential threat and consequently proposed outright amalgamation with the Lancaster & Carlisle. However, a railway shareholders' meeting in February 1846 unanimously rejected the proposal and the directors resigned. As the Lancaster & Preston Junction Act contained no provisions for the election of a new board, the railway company found itself in the astonishing position of having no directors, no means of electing new ones, and a railway that was legally leased to the Lancaster & Carlisle but in practice was in the hands of the Lancaster Canal company through an unratified lease that, strictly, was illegal. The canal company of course, was actually running the trains, although the Lancaster & Carlisle was trying hard to take them on as part of the 1844 agreement.

This chaotic state continued for four years as wrangling continued between the three parties. In November 1845, the canal informed the Lancaster & Carlisle that it would enforce the 1844 agreement from 1 January 1846, to which the Lancaster & Carlisle demanded that the Lancaster & Preston Junction be handed over to it under the terms of the 1844 lease. The canal company responded by unsuccessfully trying to obtain an injunction in the Chancery Court for enforcement of the 1842 lease. Matters worsened in September 1846 when the Lancaster & Carlisle opened its line as far as Kendal, and three months later to Carlisle, where it joined the Caledonian Railway to Glasgow. The Lancaster & Carlisle now calmly proceeded to run its trains over the Lancaster & Preston Junction line through to Preston, but refused to pay a toll to the canal company because, it said, there was no legal body to pay to. The canal company, having withdrawn its Lancaster-Preston passenger boats, continued running its own trains over the Lancaster & Preston Junction.

In February 1846, a fifth player entered the scene: the East Lancashire Railway. It was a rapidly expanding company that by taking over small local lines was in the process of connecting east Lancashire cotton towns with Manchester, Preston and Liverpool. With an eye on expanding northward it offered to buy out both the Lancaster & Preston Junction, for £29,000 outright, and the canal, for £23,500 a year, redeemable within ten years at 25 years' purchase. When agreement was close, again the Lancaster & Preston Junction Railway shareholders rebelled, forcing the East Lancashire and the canal company to break off negotiations. Once more the canal sought to enforce the 1842 lease, whereupon the railway shareholders unanimously resolved to rescind their original approval. After more bickering, the canal company tried to bring the dispute to a head by withholding the current half-year's rent, at the same time seeking support from the Lancaster & Carlisle, to which it offered to sell out, complete with the Lancaster & Preston Junction.

During this time, both companies had been running their own trains between Lancaster and Preston quite independently, with little or no regulation; government legislation in this sphere of railway operating was yet to come. Inevitably there was an accident. On 22 August 1848, a London to Glasgow express hauled by a Lancaster & Carlisle locomotive ran into the rear of a Lancaster & Preston stopping train standing in Bay Horse station south of Lancaster. One passenger was killed and several injured. At the enquiry held by the Board of Trade, the government inspector severely criticised both companies, and they were ordered to reach a proper agreement. At last all three companies behaved sensibly. In December, it was agreed that the Lancaster & Preston Junction would take back the lease to the canal for £4,875 a year for the unexpired portion, with an eighteen months option to consolidate the full sum plus 5 per cent, or 4½ per cent for any other period. For its part, the canal would withdraw its injunction application, while the Lancaster & Preston Junction undertook

The original Lancaster & Preston Junction Railway station house at Brock, with an LMS 'Royal Scot' locomotive on a southbound stopping train, c1938. (*courtesy late Douglas Thompson*)

Bay Horse station, scene of the 1848 accident, 1965.

to promote a Bill to gain parliamentary sanction. In the event, the ensuing Act went further and authorised the Lancaster & Carlisle and the Lancaster & Preston Junction to amalgamate, something they had already provisionally agreed to do, on a profit sharing basis. The Lancaster & Carlisle had to pay outstanding canal company tolls, subject to arbitration by Robert Stephenson who awarded the canal £55,552. The canal surrendered possession of the Lancaster & Preston Junction Railway on 1 August 1849, having operated it for seven years; successfully in its own view, if not in others', and certainly profitably. Meanwhile, the Kendal passenger boat service had been withdrawn and the boats broken up, excepting *Crewdson* which was re-named *Waterwitch II* and became an inspection boat.

Peace at last

Strangely the canal company's scheming and poor performance as a railway operator did little to affect its public standing. Instead, criticism was directed at the Lancaster & Preston Junction. After all, the canal profited from the affair by a total of £63,391, enabling it to redeem its mortgages of £26,000, award shareholders a bonus of £1.17.6d (£1.87½p) per share, and set up a £6,700 contingencies fund. The dividend in 1846 rose by 2 per cent to 2½, then fell to 2¼ in 1847 and '48, and to 2 per cent in 1849 and 1850. Compared with many canals these were low, but the Lancaster was relatively isolated, not connected by water to the country's main system, and in north Lancashire and Westmorland it performed a vital function in bringing in coal and taking out limestone and other minerals. It was powerful enough to induce the Lancaster & Carlisle Railway to enter into a traffic-sharing agreement in 1850, whereby the canal took the coal and heavy goods and the railway the merchandise. The canal continued trading from Glasson to Preston, and the rates for coal to Kendal and beyond were settled in a further agreement.

The canal's leading negotiator in these troubled years was B P Gregson. He had devised the successful strategy, which in 1844 was recognised by a fixed salary of £1,000 per year for the rest of his service. Even so, in 1846 he was engaged by the Edinburgh & Glasgow Railway to be its manager, no doubt on the basis of his experience of railway working gained in the previous years. That both the canal and the railway companies accepted his dual role speaks highly of his capabilities, with no reduction in salary. For some time, he had been steadily taking over his father's duties as clerk, so he must have been confident of his position when he took on the Edinburgh & Glasgow job. Indeed, the Lancaster had much for which to thank both men. Samuel continued to be the official clerk until his death in October 1846, aged 84, having devoted 54 years to the canal and promoting its business.

In this period, more attempts were made to halt the decline of Lancaster as a port. Larger ships meant that fewer could navigate the Lune as far as Glasson Dock, much less to the city's quayside. Periodically, the Ribble still threatened competition as successive ideas to improve it were made. In 1838, a second navigation company was formed to make a dock at Lytham where ships could discharge into lighters and proceed up a deepened channel to enlarged quays at Preston. As noted in Chapter 5, these works were completed in 1842, while the Preston & Wyre Railway's new port of Fleetwood introduced more competition after the railway's opening in 1840. As a counter, three proposals were made for Lancaster: one to deepen the Lune channel; another to revive the Thornbush dock scheme of 1799 with a railway to the Lancaster & Preston line at Ellel – still leased to the canal company, of course; and, most ambitious of all, docks at Poulton-le-Sands (now Morecambe) connected by a 3½ miles ship canal to the Lune at Lancaster, where the river would be dammed to make a deep-water harbour. This last proposal seems to have

The silver dissolution medal, struck in 1885.

been associated with the promotion of the 'Little' North Western Railway which was originally intended to terminate at Lancaster, where an improved port would facilitate cross-country trade with industrial West Yorkshire. The Lancaster & Carlisle Railway promised £1,600 to Lancaster merchants and £10,000 towards improving the river, in return for their support in gaining the Admiralty's consent to its building a railway bridge across the Lune.

More railway competition

The secretary of the 'Little' North Western was Edmund Sharpe, an architect and engineer prominent in Lancaster affairs.

The Tidal Harbours Commission was responsible for overseeing the spending of the £10,000, and at an enquiry in 1845 Sharpe was severely critical of the Thornbush scheme, attacking the canal company for supporting it. The canal, as Lancaster & Preston Junction leaseholder, naturally would benefit from the increased traffic going to the railway. The canal company, Sharpe said, already monopolised the city's communications, and the Thornbush proposal would be even more detrimental to the port. However, he had to admit that many ships could not get up-river, and had to discharge into canal barges at Glasson. 'Yes', he said in response to a query about

The reverse side of the dissolution medal.

the destination of transhipped cargoes at Glasson, they went by canal 'both to the town of Lancaster and the town of Preston', adding 'the traffic to the town of Preston, I fancy, is considerably more than that which comes to the town of Lancaster'. He went on to press for the ship canal scheme on the 'Little' North Western's behalf, supported by Poulton landowners, Lancaster merchants and, importantly, the large and powerful Midland Railway with which the 'Little' North Western would connect at Skipton. The Midland, of course, had an eye on the 'Little' North Western as an outlet to the west coast, and eventually acquired it outright.

The 'Little' North Western moved quickly. A Morecambe Bay Harbour Company was proposed, with a capital of £300,000 to make a harbour and a ship canal to Lancaster, but following objections from the Lancaster & Carlisle the ship canal was substituted by a railway. The Lancaster & Carlisle's support was essential in parliament, particularly in view of the £10,000 it had given for improvement of the Lune. Additionally, it was revealed that the cost of the ship canal had been under-estimated by £50,000. After more argument, a Bill for a harbour and railway was presented to parliament and in 1846 the Morecambe Harbour & Railway Act was passed. The Lune was

The Fishergate tramroad tunnel in 1986, used as an entrance to a car park.

deepened, helped by the Lancaster & Carlisle's money, but the improvement was only temporary as the superior advantages of a port at Morecambe, in the shape of a stone jetty into the bay, became apparent, and the decline of Lancaster as a port was accelerated. The 'Little' North Western quickly exercised its option to purchase the harbour company, and after the combined concern was acquired by the Midland further improvements were made, culminating in 1904 with a new deep-water harbour at Heysham. The effect of these developments on the Lancaster Canal was negligible. Although in 1849 a connecting curve was made at Lancaster from the 'Little' North Western to the Lancaster & Carlisle, the traffic on the 'Little' North Western essentially

was east and west and the new port at Morecambe barely affected the trade through Glasson.

Shortly after the Kendal & Windermere Railway was opened in 1847, the canal company opened negotiations for a tramroad from the canal head to Kendal station, but they were abortive and coal continued to be taken between the two by road. In 1851, the Lancaster leased merchandise tolls on the South End of the canal for 21 years to the Leeds & Liverpool. The South End, it will be remembered, now formed that company's line from Johnson's Hillock to Wigan. In return, it paid the Lancaster £4,335 a year, and the Lancaster retained coal and minerals traffic bound for the tramroad and the North End, traffic on which the

Lancaster & Carlisle Railway was making inroads, particularly that from Glasson. The canal offered reduced rates for coal, and in February that year decided to start its own trading in coastal traffic. The company purchased a schooner *Woodbine*, then in 1852 *Richard* – which six months later was lost in the Duddon estuary – followed by *Oriental* and, in 1853, *Bloomer*. Three more were bought in 1855, making a fleet of six. It also tried out a steamer, *Dandy*, but did not keep it. The consequent increase in the coal trade through Glasson and the renting of a quay at Belfast, working through a local agent, improved the company's fortunes, but they did not last long and income from Glasson resumed its decline.

The railway takes over

Relations with the Lancaster & Carlisle Railway were cool but not antagonistic. In 1853, the railway company discovered that the canal was carrying pig iron and treacle from Glasgow, brought coastwise into Glasson and bound for Preston, at very low rates. This was considered to contravene the competition agreement, so the canal company obligingly opened its books for inspection. After another infringement was suspected but independently verified as unproven, all seemed well until September 1858 when the Lancaster & Carlisle suddenly announced that it was repudiating the agreement because of the pig iron and treacle episode five years previously.

It seems probable that it was heavily influenced by the London & North Western Railway, a powerful company that controlled the line from London to Preston, had helped to finance the Lancaster & Carlisle, and had seven representatives on the board. It was an aggressive company which twelve months later leased the Lancaster & Carlisle giving it total control from London to Carlisle. In an effort to gain new traffic, the canal company hired the Lancaster Steam Navigation Company's steamer *Duchess*, sailing twice weekly between Glasson and Liverpool carrying merchandise at £37.10s (£37.50) per trip. A steam tug for the canal was built to order, followed by two more second-hand in June 1860, but after only a few years haulage reverted to horses. Adversely, the coastal vessels were lost at sea in June 1860, leaving only *Woodbine* in service, but not for long. A general economic depression added to the canal's troubles, resulting in a fall in dividend, which since 1851 had been stable at £1.15s (£1.75p) per £100 share, to £1.12s (£1.60p) in 1863.

By this time, control of the tramroad had passed to the North Union Railway after it amalgamated with the Bolton & Preston in 1844, which in turn became jointly owned by the London & North Western and Lancashire & Yorkshire railways, thereby acquiring the lease from the canal company, giving them responsibility for maintaining the Ribble tramroad bridge, which by 1856 had been twice repaired. The joint lessees continually squabbled over its costs – in 1856 amounting to £1,500 – and eventually sought the canal company's consent to closing that part of the tramroad to avoid having to completely rebuild it. Naturally the canal insisted on keeping to the 1837 agreement. Meanwhile the Avenham incline engine boiler had to be renewed in 1858, costing £120.

In September 1860, the canal company sought to lease itself to the London & North Western. After two years of negotiations, a Bill was presented to parliament only to be opposed by the Lancashire & Yorkshire which wanted a share in any lease. The London & North Western Railway withdrew its Bill, but tried again, successfully, in the next session, resulting in the Lancaster Canal Transfer Act of 29 July 1864. It authorised the lease of the North End of the canal to the London & North Western Railway in perpetuity for £12,665.17s.6d (£12,665. 87½p) a year, and the South End likewise to the Leeds & Liverpool for £7,075. That company in the meantime had leased the tolls on its own canal to a consortium of three railways. The Act also authorised increased maximum tolls on both ends. The canal company considered it had made a good bargain, ridding itself of an increasingly falling asset in return for a guaranteed income.

Rental from the lease enabled a return to a dividend of £1.15s (£1.75p) per cent, and added income was secured by investing the company's cash balance of £18,239. These continued until 1885 when the London & North Western offered outright purchase in exchange for 4 per cent railway debenture stock equal to the rent the canal was receiving from the leases on both ends, representing £43.15s (£43.75p) per share, which the shareholders accepted. Despite opposition from Lancaster Corporation, the Lancaster Shipping Company and the Lancaster Port Commissioners, the canal was duly acquired by the railway company by an Act of 16 July 1885, including the 1864 lease of the South End to the Leeds & Liverpool and the carrying business, as from 1 July. However, the canal company was not formally wound up until 1 January 1886, the shareholders each receiving a bonus of 10s 9d. (54p). The remaining cash balance was handed to the chairman, who used it to strike a number of commemorative silver medallions.

Back in 1864, the little-used section of the tramroad from Bamber Bridge to Preston had been closed and the land sold, leaving only the Walton Summit-Bamber Bridge length in use for supplying coal to mills there. Eventually this section, too, was closed under a London & North Western Railway Act of 1879, all traffic having ceased. The tramplates were taken up and sold for scrap, although some remained in Fishergate tunnel until 1884, after which it was partly filled in. The remainder was enlarged to form an entrance to the Lancashire & Yorkshire Railway's new goods station in Butler Street, which in turn was closed in 1971 and is now the site of a multi-storey car park and shopping centre. The course of the tramroad from Penwortham to what is now Avenham Park passed to Preston Corporation, which in 1963 rebuilt the Ribble bridge in reinforced concrete but retained the original design.

Bryan Padgett Gregson died on 3 December 1872, having served the canal company for sixty years. At the 1865 shareholders' annual meeting, following the Transfer Act, he made a long statement setting out the history of the canal during that time, concluding by thanking the committee for its support. Like his father and elder brother Samuel II – who had been the city's MP – Bryan Padgett was prominent in local affairs, including being a Deputy Lieutenant of Lancashire. He had served the company well, and after the chairman hastily withdrew a proposal to award him a flat sum of £4,500 the shareholders resolved to give him an annuity of £1,000 a year in recognition of his long service. Indeed, without his sagacity, tenacity and foresight the canal company would have been lost to the railways long before.

CHAPTER 7

RAILWAY CONTROL AND AFTER

Continuing Prosperity

When the North Union Railway was opened to Preston a short branch was made to the canal basin. Under London & North Western ownership, additional wharves and sidings were built, and the site became a busy railway and canal interchange for coal going north and minerals coming south. The extent of the wharves at Preston and Kendal compared with Lancaster is indicative of their relative importance to the canal, which continued to be a dominant force in the economy of north Lancashire and Westmorland. A railway company land plan of 1880 shows numerous public wharves, coal yards, and various canal-side or adjacent industries. They included eight cotton mills at Preston, four at Lancaster and a woollen mill at Kendal, among lime kilns, coke ovens, quarries, brick works, corn mills and foundries, to name a few. Kendal corporation's large warehouse at the end of the basin had been closed off by this time to become an ironworks, later much extended.

A variety of imports came in through Glasson, including minerals, grain and timber. Chemicals came in for Wakefields' gunpowder mills at Sedgwick, south of Kendal, and after new mills were opened at Gatebeck in 1850 a new wharf was made at Crooklands whence they were conveyed to the mills along a 5-mile horse tramway. After the tramway was extended along the roadside to Milnthorpe station in 1876 powder went out by rail, although coal for the mills was still brought in by canal.

The canal to Glasson Dock still continued to be important even after the

London & North Western Railway opened a branch line to it from Lancaster in 1883. In 1894, for instance, it was still the cheapest route for heavy goods to Kendal, and cement for building the dam across Thirlmere that turned it into a reservoir for Manchester's water. Consequently, the London & North Western Railway

The canal and railway interchange at Preston in 1944.

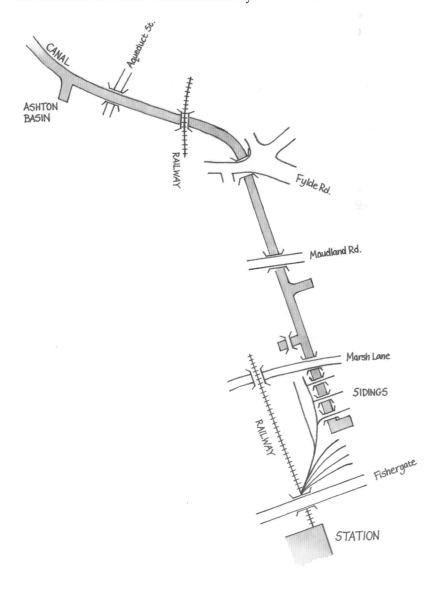

Old canal toll and weighbridge house on the corner of Marsh Lane and Ladywell St., Preston, 1954.

A later view from the other side, 1963.

A canal warehouse in Corporation St., Preston, 1954.

Preston basin after closure, looking south, c1960.

Preston basin, looking north, c1950.

kept up a good standard of maintenance, under a canal superintendent based at Lancaster Castle station. Revenue in 1888 was £17,289; in 1905 it was £13,984, a modest fall considering that canals generally by then were rapidly becoming to be considered an outmoded form of transport.

Apart from a steam ice-breaker and a dredger, haulage was still by horses. For a short period after 1918, a pair of Leeds & Liverpool steam tugs were tried, but, as in 1860, the Lancaster's shallower depth made them uneconomic because barges could not be as fully laden as in the past. In 1921, they were returned to the

Leeds & Liverpool by sea from Glasson to the Douglas, the same route as that by which they had arrived. After the last boat builder in Lancaster closed, all new craft on the canal came that way.

Progressive Closure

When the railways were grouped into four large companies in 1923, the London & North Western became part of the London Midland & Scottish Railway, which company in 1935 gained an Act to permit the raising of canal tolls. In 1939, a further Act empowered the London Midland & Scottish to close the last half-mile from Kendal gas works to Canal

Coal being discharged on a railway wagon tippler at Preston, c1923.

Head because of leakages in the canal bed, a recurring problem since early days. However, it did not take place until 1941-2. Then in 1944, the London Midland & Scottish promoted a Bill to close a number of its canals, including the Lancaster, but opposition from firms in Lancaster, from Kendal borough council, and the gas works, all reliant on the canal for coal, succeeded in having the Lancaster deleted from the Bill. The gas works alone was receiving up to 7,500 tons of coal a year. However, perhaps seeing the writing on the wall, the gas works went over to receiving its coal by rail and thence by road from the station, marking the end of commercial traffic north of Lancaster. Three years later, in 1947, the last traffic was carried from Preston to Lancaster, again coal.

Nationalisation

In 1948, most of Britain's canal system was nationalised and the Lancaster became part of the Docks & Inland Waterways Executive of the British Transport Commission. Later the Transport Act of 1953 gave the commission discretion to close a number of disused or little-used canals. Subsequently about 5¾ miles from Stainton Crossings bridge to Kendal were drained because of continual leakages through limestone fissures in the bed, and the last two miles were filled in and sold to adjoining landowners. The towing path and its site were declared a public footpath. At Preston, some ¾ mile south from Aqueduct Street was drained and progressively sold over the ensuing years. At the end of 1962, the commission was dissolved and in January 1963 canals were placed under an autonomous British Waterways Board reporting directly to the Minister of Transport. Meanwhile the canal from Tewitfield Locks to Stainton was officially closed and 'ponded', that is it retained water to a depth of 2ft 6in–3ft

6in in order to maintain the flow from feeders from Stainton Beck, Peasey Beck at Crooklands – which brought water down from Killington Reservoir – and Farleton Beck. There was another feeder from the River Calder at Garstang. The flow to the canal above Tewitfield was important because a profit was made from supplying water. Pipelines led to railway water troughs for steam locomotives at Brock and Hest Bank, to engine sheds at Carnforth and Preston, a number of industrial premises, particularly at Lancaster and Preston, a chemical works at Fleetwood, and the UK Atomic Energy works near Salwick.

Pleasure craft were increasingly being brought on to the canal, generally of narrow boat dimensions, and in 1956 the Lancaster Canal Boat Club was formed. But even though there was still sufficient depth above Tewitfield, very few ventured up the locks which steadily became dilapidated. Eventually the gates were removed and concrete sills were installed to act as weirs. Furthermore, 100yd of ponded canal near Holme was drained and replaced by iron pipes. Some years later they in turn were replaced by a concrete channel or 'flume', and thanks to a far-sighted British Waterways Area Engineer it was made wide and deep enough for a standard narrow boat, thus anticipating possible future use by pleasure craft, even though isolated from the main canal. This now comprised 47 miles of level, navigable waterway from Preston to Tewitfield, and the 2¾ miles–long Glasson branch with six locks; the state of the canal as it is today.

Blocking the Northern Reaches

In 1965, government legislation authorised an extension of the M6 motorway northward from Carnforth. It was planned to cross the ponded section, or the Northern Reaches as they became known, at six places, including associated roads that were to be re-routed. Only small box

The iron pipe under the filled-in section at Holme, 1971.

The same view after the pipe was replaced by a navigable concrete flume, 1988.

culverts were built, just large enough to take the water flow but no more. Consequently, again the Northern Reaches would be severed, this time into seven sections. Further, a new Kendal link road, A590, would cross the drained section by an embankment just east of Hincaster tunnel near Sedgwick, at an acute angle. The work aroused fierce opposition from the boat club, the anglers' association, other users and environmentalists. In December 1963, the Association for the Restoration of the Lancaster Canal was formed, later renamed the Lancaster Canal Trust, but regrettably their combined efforts had no effect.

The work of the trust will be outlined more fully in Chapter 9, but to complete the canal's history the success in restoring and re-opening Ashton Basin as a marina at Preston in 1972 should

be mentioned here. Finally, in 2002, the Lancaster Canal was at last connected to the country's main network by water. Some three miles of the Savick Brook at Haslam Park, Preston, were widened and partly straightened to make the 'Ribble Link' to the river estuary two miles downstream from Preston Dock, capable of taking boats of 2ft draught. It falls by nine locks to the river at Lea Marsh, where craft can proceed upstream to Preston Dock, then down the other side to the River Douglas, and thence on to the Leeds & Liverpool Canal. The Lancaster Canal Boat Club promoted the scheme, a separate trust was set up including representation from the Lancaster Canal Trust and other interested parties, and the link was made with funding from the Millennium Lottery Fund.

The Ribble Link
The junction at Ingol, Preston, 2007.

The two-rise locks at the head of the link, showing Savick Brook entering on the left and the commemorative statue at the top, now removed, 2007.

Railway bridge over the link, originally built to take the brook, 2007.

Ribble Link Lock no. 8, 2007.

Northern Reaches culvert under North Road, Holme, 1994.

Looking north to Crooklands Bridge from the M6, with the top of Millness culvert in the foreground.

The canal culverted under the M6 motorway, looking from Millness Bridge, Crooklands, 1971.

CHAPTER 8

THE CANAL TODAY

The South End

Of the three historic sections of canal – the South End and tramroad, the navigable 42 miles from Preston to Tewitfield, and the Northern Reaches – the first has changed the most since nationalisation in 1948, although the large wharf at Botany Bay, or Knowley as it was also known, still contains a derelict cottage and stable for boat horses. After the South End was incorporated into the Leeds & Liverpool, the stretch northward from Johnson's Hillock became that company's Walton Summit branch. Until the late 1940s, it continued in declining use, serving several wharves, limekilns and small waterside industries such as a mordant works near Rip Row making a chemical used in dyeing. Now, all that remains is a short stretch containing water at Johnson's Hillock, the two short Whittle Hills tunnels and the deep cutting between them, an overbridge immediately beyond, and the small River Lostock aqueduct. The bridge carries a plaque erected in 2003 to commemorate the bi-centenary of the opening of this part of the canal. Further on, the canal and the tramroad to a point west of Bamber Bridge have been obliterated by housing and industrial development that followed the establishment of the Central Lancashire New Town Corporation, although the area is still known as Walton Summit.

From what was the top of the Penwortham incline at Carr Wood, the tramroad site is a public footpath, crossing the valley on a low embankment to the Ribble at the Old Tram Bridge, as it is still known, and up the former incline into Avenham Park. The site of the canal basins and wharves at Preston were filled in from 1962 onward and have long been redeveloped. Apart from an iron bridge parapet in Marsh Lane there is now no evidence of the canal until its present terminus beyond the site of Tulketh aqueduct over the appropriately named Aqueduct Street, south of Ashton Basin.

Preston to Tewitfield

The canal-side environment has been changed by housing development at several places, notably Preston and Hest Bank, although overall the section from Preston to Lancaster and Tewitfield has, in proportion to its length, probably changed the least, apart from the junction with the Ribble Link.

Distances on the milestones run from Preston to Garstang, Garstang to Lancaster and Lancaster to Kendal. Rennie's hump-backed bridges are landmarks, with more modern additions in places, such as that under the Garstang by-pass road. All the originals have names, but under British Waterways ownership they were numbered as well, indicated by cast metal plates. Three bridges are of particular interest, all in the last five miles to Lancaster. Ellel Grange bridge, No. 84, is a standard Rennie design but with elegant balustraded parapets to dignify the private drive to the grange. The next bridge, No. 85, is appropriately named Double bridge because it is twice the normal width and has a third parapet or wall down the middle. It is sited on the boundary between two land ownerships and was placed there to provide separate access over a single structure to save the expense of two separate bridges. Brantbeck bridge, No. 91, is a particularly tall one at the south end of Burrow Heights cutting, more popularly known as 'Deep Cutting', over 30ft deep and 1½ miles long. There were also three wooden swing bridges over the canal, at Lea – No. 20, and now demolished – Hollowforth, No. 37, and north of Lancaster, Hatlex at Hest Bank, No. 120, both now replaced by steel bridges. Features of many of the bridges are clumps of larch trees, planted partly to stabilise the banks and also to provide timber for stop planks and other purposes. The aqueducts and syphons have already been mentioned in Chapter 2.

There are numerous moorings and several marinas along the canal, indicative of its popularity for boating. A former stable block and cottages at Swillbrook bridge, No. 32, and Salwick wharf (bridge 24) near Catforth, have been modernised, the latter with a boatyard for hire craft. There is also a large marina at Moons bridge (36) with two new basins. The former wharf cottages and stable at Stubbins bridge (51), Catterall, have been enlarged as a house. Garstang basin contains moorings, and there is a long-established marina at Galgate, close to the junction with the Glasson branch. Alongside lock No. 6 on the branch, Thurnham Mill has lost the interest it had. Its original wheel – replaced later by a water turbine – was turned by water taken from the canal, as described in Chapter 5. However, in recent years it has been assimilated into a new hotel complex and is no longer recognisable, while its distinctive water supply features have almost disappeared. Close to Ratcliffe Wharf (bridge 75) at Forton, a large limekiln stands in a garden.

The canal through Lancaster has seen many changes, particularly at the old wharves near Penny Street bridge. The passenger boat house on the east bank has been converted into high-class flats, together with the adjacent workshops and warehouse, while the old stables and cottages have long been a pub. On the opposite bank, two large basins, once partly roofed over, are now flanked by more flats owned by Lancaster University. The entire area has been transformed. Just beyond Penny Street bridge on the east

bank, canal-side mills have been converted for other purposes. The original 'Packet Station' was here. There is still a former dry dock next to the bridge of that name, No. 103, now very overgrown.

Once out of the city the canal crosses Caton Road on the concrete Bulk aqueduct. Immediately following, it crosses the magnificent Lune aqueduct. Just short of Hest Bank the canal runs close to the coast, where transhipments took place at the Hest Bank Shipping Company's wharf. The 1847 Ordnance Survey map shows a breakwater enclosing part of the bay near the Keer channel, and at low tides the remains of a stone pier are sometimes revealed. Cargoes were transferred by cart to and from the canal wharf. At Bolton-le-Sands the Packet Boat pub is a reminder of the canal's importance to the area. Bolton Cinder Oven bridge, No. 125, also is a reminder of a past industry.

Carnforth wharf, where today there are extensive moorings and a marina, was used for loading barges with gravel from nearby pits. Near here, a series of coke ovens on the east side are being restored by the Friends of Carnforth Coke Ovens as a local industrial heritage site; the best preserved of several along the North End. Little more than a mile from Tewitfield, just before reaching Capernwray, the deep Over Head Quarry on the east side was connected to the canal by a short tramway that carried limestone to a wharf. The quarry itself is now a diving and underwater swimming centre. Capernwray bridge, no. 131, precedes the Keer aqueduct alongside Capernwray Mill on the towing path side of the canal, described in Chapter 2. The mill took water from the River Keer upstream of the canal, along a headrace channel which passed through the embankment in a pipe that discharged on to the overshot wheel via a wooden trough. Part of the wheel has been preserved as a feature. The aqueduct also has an overflow pipe on the opposite, east, side, no longer used but with the remains of a sluice gate mechanism inside the parapet. The pipe was replaced by a concrete spillway just south of the aqueduct. As recently as 2002, the 2½in Ordnance Survey map showed the course of a feeder channel on the east side of the canal, winding across fields for just over a mile, from the river at Keer Bridge alongside Capernwray Park. However, all that remained of it in 2016 appears to be the arch of a culvert leading into the canal at Capernwray bridge, and a stone abutment where it crossed Swarth Beck, presumably by an aqueduct which could have been merely a wooden trough.

After the aqueduct, a 100yd arm of the canal leads into another large quarry once forming extensive limestone workings and now a large static caravan park. The remains of a stone loading platform and crane near the entrance were served by a short tramway. Nearby, a row of workers' houses, New England Cottages, was demolished in the 1980s.

The end of navigation is at the first of the box culverts immediately at the foot of the eight Tewitfield locks. Beyond them the only boats on the canal are small dinghies and similar craft that can be brought by road to the sections between the culverts. The Tewitfield culvert passes beneath the M6 and the A6070 road, which was rebuilt as part of the construction of the adjoining motorway. There are moorings and other facilities here, where the canal takes a sharp right-hand bend before terminating at the culvert. Straight on is a short arm that ends at the motorway and the A6070, beyond which a shallow, overgrown cutting can be seen running west for about 100 yards. It may have been the beginning of Rennie's original line which he planned to run in that direction. Alternatively, it may be evidence that work was started on the planned Warton Crag branch, but was not completed.

The termination of the canal at Preston, 1971, with the entrance to Ashton Basin on the right.

Tewitfield No. 6 lock, 1968.

The end of the navigable canal at Tewitfield, 1971.

The ornamental bridge at Ellel Grange, 1985.

Double Bridge, 1969.

Brantbeck or Deep
Cutting Bridge, 1980.

Garstang Basin after development as a marina, with the old warehouse on the left converted to a restaurant, 2008.

Galgate Marina and extensive canal-side moorings, 1995.

The abandoned cutting at Tewitfield, 1989.

The Northern Reaches

Paradoxically, the splitting of the nine miles of canal to Stainton into relatively short sections between the box culverts has meant that otherwise it has changed very little since 1968. There are no series of permanent moorings, as there are to the south, and one of the several wharves is still used, but served by road for other purposes. Beyond Stainton, of course, the canal is dry or has been filled in.

At the village of Burton-in-Kendal there are two more interesting aqueducts, each taking a road under the canal by a tunnel in the embankment. Burton Road aqueduct has a low segmental arch, next to a wharf and former cottage; New Mill aqueduct is taller and round-headed.

At Holme, there is a series of Rennie-type bridges close together.

Approaching Farleton, the M6 again severs the canal just short of Duke's bridge, No. 155, which unusually has a separate low arch, acting as a 'cattle creep' to connect severed land. Immediately past it, Farleton basin is opposite an extensive wharf flanked by a former warehouse and stable, now roofless. A two-storey building at the foot of an embankment, with the upper floor at water level, it is approached by a grassy lane alongside the canal from Farleton Turnpike bridge, No. 156, on the A6070 beneath Farleton Knott, a prominent limestone fell which had quarries and lime kilns. It was obviously a busy place for transhipping to canal barges.

Farleton aqueduct takes Farleton Beck under the canal, followed by a feeder from an upstream weir. In another mile, Moss Side bridge, carrying the A65 road, has been culverted, followed by the last box culvert, under the M6 at Millness. Here there is an extensive wharf, a double-arched aqueduct and a feeder from Peasey Beck. Crooklands bridge, No. 166, adjoins Wakefields' wharf, once serving their gunpowder mills, close to the wharf used by the Lancaster Canal Trust for its trip-boat operations. A brief history of the site and the gunpowder works tramway is displayed on an information panel. The wharf includes a canal boat stable, acquired by the trust and restored for use as a store, complete with wooden boskins that made stalls for two horses.

In little more than a mile, Stainton aqueduct crosses the beck of that name, from which runs the final feeder. Just beyond, at Stainton Crossings bridge, no. 172, the canal was drained until,

in 2015, volunteers working under the auspices of the trust extended the watered section some 200yd to the next bridge, Sellet Hall. Five hundred yards further on the canal bed is severed by the A590 Kendal link road, built at the same time as the M6. It also swallowed up Wellhead bridge. The canal here runs due west, and almost immediately enters Hincaster tunnel, while the towing path takes its own course in a narrow cutting over the hill. Iron rings that supported the hauling chain can be seen inside the tunnel, which still holds shallow water.

At the other end, a sharp right-hand turn takes the canal northward again at Hincaster wharf, where a former warehouse has been converted into dwellings. Thereafter the canal is either dry or has been completely taken into adjoining land, in two places leaving bridges isolated in fields. The canal is again severed by the A590 in a deep cutting at an acute angle, some 500yd long,

The curiously-named Stainton Bridge End Bridge, 1977.

The end of the Northern Reaches still in water at Stainton Crossings Bridge, 1989.

North of Stainton only the old towing path remains as a public footpath, with Natland Hall Bridge now standing in a field, 1977.

Kendal's Zion Sunday School outing to Sedgwick passing under Kendal Changeline Bridge, early 1900s. (*courtesy Kendal Library*)

The same bridge in 2009.

Skating on the frozen canal c1910, near Highgate Settlings bridge (Burton Road), now filled in. (*courtesy Kendal Library*)

Kendal Castle (or Parr St.) Bridge, showing 1888 widening, 1976.

Pleasure boating at the head of the Glasson branch, Galgate, 1964.

Hincaster warehouse, converted into dwellings, 1991.

Capernwray Mill in
1967. Water for the
overshot wheel was
delivered from the
River Keer through a
pipe under the canal
and on to a wooden
trough leading from
the square hole in the
embankment wall.

Overflow from the
canal at Capernwray
Aqueduct, 1967.

Capernwray Mill restored as a house, 1978. (*J S Gavan*)

The canal side of Holme Mills, which the canal once served, 1990.

The end of the watered section of the Northern Reaches in 1968.

Larkrigg Hall Bridge, 1977.

Crow Park Bridge, 1968.

Natland Road Bridge,
now demolished, 1953.

The course of the
canal looking south
near the site of Natland
Road Bridge, 1977.

The warehouse at Canal Head, Kendal, has long been concealed by later extensions, but the small building on the left probably was the original packet boat office, 1976.

The interior of Gilkes' works at Canal Head, showing the original arches over the canal arms, 2017. (*P. Aitken*)

involving towing path walkers in a signposted detour. It then passes through Sedgwick village on an embankment and a slightly skewed road aqueduct having a similar arch profile to Burton Road aqueduct at Holme. From Natland, the canal has been completely filled in, including Natland Road and Highgate Settlings (Burton Road, A65) bridges. Here it enters Kendal and is a footpath and cycle way. At Changeline bridge the towing path moves to the east side. The bridge is of ingenious design, common on many canals, enabling barge horses to cross from one side to the other without detaching the towline. From here the western side is lined with various industrial premises, including the former gas and electricity works. Parkside Road bridge has been demolished. The termination of the canal at Canal Head comprised a large basin running off the western side at a slightly acute angle, ending at a two-storey warehouse which barges could enter through two arched openings, now incorporated into the premises of Gilbert Gilkes & Gordon, founded in 1881, pump and turbine manufacturers, and originally known as Canal Iron Works. A small building on the north side is thought to have been the original ticket office for the passenger boat service. The present chairman of Gilkes, C.W.N. Crewdson, OBE, is a descendant of the Crewdsons who were original canal company directors, thereby maintaining a family connection with the canal from its earliest days.

CHAPTER 9

TOWARDS RESTORATION?

The volunteer movement

In 1946 the Inland Waterways Association was founded. The Second World War had ended in the previous year and after a temporary war-time revival the canal system as a means of commercial transport resumed its rapid decline. But some people saw canals as a means of recreation and as an environmental and heritage asset that should be retained and, where necessary, restored. The formation of a national voluntary body to promote these objectives encouraged the growth of regional canal societies affiliated to it, focusing on local waterways. Despite at first having no support from the Docks & Inland Waterways Executive, during the next fifty years some remarkable restoration projects were achieved, largely using voluntary labour, although, after the British Waterways Board was set up, there was a gradual softening of official attitudes, joint projects began to be undertaken, and there were no more closures. In 2010, the Board was replaced by an independent charity, the Canal & River Trust, with representatives of all interested parties, including the IWA.

The end of an I.W.A. towing path walk on the Northern Reaches, Canal Head, Kendal, 1977.

An I.W.A. cruise at Lancaster, 1977.

The founder and first secretary of the Lancaster Canal Trust (originally called the Association for the Restoration of the Lancaster Canal) in 1963 was T.S.H. Wordsworth, a planning department official with Lancashire County Council. The committee included representatives from the Ramblers Association, the Lancashire Naturalists Trust, Lancashire Rural Studies Association, the Lancaster Canal Boat Club, the Northern Anglers Association and commercial boat hirers.

Campaigning for the Northern Reaches

Details of the government's intention to extend the M6 motorway through Cumbria were published in 1964. The proposed culverts described in Chapter 8

would, of course, destroy any prospect of restoring the Northern Reaches, and the trust, together with the IWA and the boat club, began a tremendous and widely-publicised campaign to retain them intact, although British Waterways and local authorities kept what can best be described as a neutral stance. A petition to the Ministry of Transport, asking for the M6 to be re-routed, delivered personally by a group of members, was politely rejected, as was a formal objection to the relevant section of the parliamentary Bill. British Waterways was persuaded to include the Lancaster in one of its series of waterways guides, but did not include the Northern Reaches.

The trust's representations for re-routing the motorway having failed, it responded with a counter-proposal to increase the size of the culverts. The extra cost was calculated at £91,000, not an over-large sum compared with the total estimate of £240,000 for the culverts, but this, too, failed and the Bill duly passed into law in 1965. However, in 1966 a minor battle was won in defeating a proposal for a narrow bridge under the M6 just below Kellet Lane bridge south of Tewitfield, instead of full barge width. It allowed all craft to navigate to the foot of the locks, where moorings and various amenities were established. That year also saw the trust organise its first public cruise in former boatman Dan Ashcroft's converted Leeds & Liverpool barge *Shelagh*. For several years he had been running public cruises at the Preston end of the canal. A particularly popular trust cruise was from Garstang to the Lune aqueduct, returning to Lancaster where a bus took passengers back to Garstang. They became regular summer attractions until Dan retired from a lifetime on the canal.

Around this time another cruise operator from Lancaster ran the former barge *Pet* under a new name, *Lady Fiona*. She had been converted into a canal dredger and loaded with concrete as ballast, which made her slow and unwieldy, and eventually she was acquired by British Waterways and taken to the Shropshire Union Canal at Nantwich. Later the Board had ideas about using her as a static exhibit to publicise the canal on land at Kendal, but after the concrete was removed the iron hull was so badly corroded that the boat was unusable.

A Lancaster Canal
Trust cruise aboard Dan Ashcroft's converted barge *Shelagh* at Glasson No. 2 lock, 1970.

A Lancaster Canal Trust cruise aboard *Shelagh* approaching Hatlex swing bridge, Hest Bank, 1968.

A maintenance boat accompanying a Lancaster Canal Trust working party on towing path clearance in Aldcliffe cutting, Lancaster, 1970.

A cast iron notice prohibiting unauthorised fishing, ratting and digging up the soil at Thurnham lock on the Glasson Dock branch, 1963.

Lancaster Canal Trust and Boat Club rally at Ashton Basin, Preston, 1970.

Ashton Basin, before restoration, 1971.

Official reopening of Ashton Basin, 1972.

A milestone near
Hincaster, 1991.

A milestone at the Lune Aqueduct after restoration by the Lancaster Canal Trust: 25 miles to Kendal, 1971.

The restored Ashton Basin, 1973.

Another restored milestone at Ingol, Preston, 1971.

Modern housing development at Ingol, Preston, showing the Trust's restored milestone, 1971.

Queen's Silver Jubilee Cruise, Lancaster Castle to Windsor Castle, 12 June 1977

The boat that carried the message to Preston, before its overland journey to the Leeds & Liverpool Canal for an onward voyage to Windsor.

The Mayor of Lancaster handing over loyal greetings to be delivered to the Queen by canal.

The Lancaster Canal
cavalcade setting off
southward.

As well as campaigning, the committee was busy organising regular working parties to clear overgrown parts of the towing path. Then in 1965 the trust published a 36-page booklet *The Lancaster Canal Proposed Linear Park and Nature Reserve*. It was virtually Wordsworth's own work, containing many sensible, well thought-out and costed proposals that today would be environmentally very praiseworthy. Unfortunately, some thought he spoiled his case by going beyond reality in recommending two entirely new canals, one nine miles long from Sedgwick up the Lyth Valley to Windermere lake, including a mile-long tunnel. The other was a thirteen-mile canal from the Lancaster a little north of Preston to the Leeds & Liverpool Canal at Riley Green, between Blackburn and Chorley, including an aqueduct across the Ribble. A third, mercifully short, connection to the Ribble below Preston was also included; a feasible suggestion which in 2002 materialised as the Ribble Link.

The booklet was received not without criticism from members, including some of the committee, particularly as its production costs severely depleted the trust's funds.

The main task now was to attract new members and restore finances. To mark the 150th anniversary of the completion of the canal to Kendal, a renewed publicity campaign began, including a celebratory exhibition in the Harris Library, Preston. Largely as a result of losing the Northern Reaches campaign, Wordsworth resigned from the committee at that year's annual meeting, to be succeeded by David Slater, who later became a long-serving chairman of the trust. In 1970, he and committee member John Gavan researched old Ordnance Survey maps to locate the canal's original milestones. Some were very hard to find on the ground, and a number were restored.

Improving the canal's environment

Early in 1970, the recently-formed Central Lancashire New Town Corporation proposed to abandon and fill in more of the canal at Preston, from Aqueduct Street to Woodplumpton Road bridge, including Ashton Basin which was very overgrown. The trust, the Boat Club and Preston Borough Council, with support from British Waterways, combined to campaign against the scheme, gaining widespread support. As a result, the British Waterways Board was able to restore the basin, with Preston Council contributing to the cost of landscaping. The basin was leased as a marina, and was re-opened with some ceremony in September 1972.

The next aim was to restore the derelict and roofless passenger packet boat house at Lancaster. As a first step, the city council listed it Grade II, and with the trust persuaded the Waterways Board to put the building into good order. It was an interesting building, two storeys high with an internal hoist for lifting boats out of the water and up to the first floor where maintenance and repair work could be undertaken. Subsequently the adjacent stable block was converted into a canalside pub.

Around this time the trust arranged a permanent exhibition of historic canal artefacts in 'Th'owd Tithe Barn' restaurant alongside Garstang basin. It was a popular feature for many years until the premises changed hands, when the exhibits were presented to the Maritime Museum at Lancaster.

In 1991, the trust organised a group of volunteers to clear the approaches to Hincaster tunnel, including the horse-path over the top. It comprised trust members, volunteer labour from the Waterways Recovery Group, and a gang from Lancaster prison. Representations by the trust succeeded in having the tunnel portals and three small bridges over the horse-path listed Grade II. One of the bridges carries the west coast main line railway; the other two connected land severed by the path, which itself, with its retaining walls, is somewhat curiously scheduled as an Ancient Monument. British Waterways placed a plaque on the western portal which incorrectly states that the tunnel is an Ancient Monument. A detachment of Royal Engineers cleared and restored the tunnel portals as a training exercise. They also inspected the interior, which was pronounced to be remarkably sound. Working parties on the horse-path continue today in conjunction with Historic England.

In 1992 and again in 2005-6, in conjunction with the Waterways Recovery Group, the Tewitfield lock walls and by-washes were repaired.

The trust erected signposts directing walkers along the canal, designated the 'Northern Reaches Trail' in 2008; some twenty all told along the towing path and at roadside locations leading to it, together with information panels and, in 2011, a number of public benches.

Hincaster Tunnel Clearance work 1968

The tunnel horsepath before the Trust began work.

The same view in 1980.

The east end of the tunnel from Wellheads Bridge (now demolished), before work commenced, 1968.

A similar view in 1988.

A close-up of the tunnel entrance, 1968.

Plaque on Hincaster Tunnel, 2001.

HINCASTER
TUNNEL
THIS WAS BUILT TO TAKE THE
LANCASTER CANAL CLOSE TO
SEDGWICK GUNPOWDER WORKS.
378 YARDS IN LENGTH, THE TUNNEL
WAS OPENED FOR USE ON THE 18TH
OF JUNE 1819.

ANCIENT MONUMENT

The former boat stable at Crooklands, derelict in 1989.

Crooklands Stable Restoration

The interior, 1991.

Passenger boats and rallies

In 1973, the trust bought its first passenger-carrying boat, *Ebb & Flow*, for short public summer cruises on the Northern Reaches from Crooklands. It was a 'hypozomatic' boat in two sections, enabling it to be dismantled for easy transportation. In 1996, it was replaced by a more conventional trip boat, named *Waterwitch* after the old canal company packet boat. It carries twelve passengers. The cruises are very popular, particularly with visitors to the Westmorland County Agricultural Society's Showground adjacent to the canal. The first Easter dinghy rally on the Northern Reaches was held at Holme in 1974, thereafter becoming a popular annual event.

In the late 1990s, the Lancaster Canal Regeneration Partnership was formed by a consortium of local authorities along the canal, the trust, Cumbria Tourism, the Friends of the Lake District and other interested bodies; part of a drive to ease pressures of tourism in the Lake District by popularising areas on its fringes, in this case restoring and popularising the towing path along the Northern Reaches for walking and cycling particularly between Natland and Kendal. A firm of consulting engineers reported on restoration of the Northern Reaches. In 2016 a part-time project manager was appointed.

The Future: a personal view

The Lancaster Canal Trust's plans for restoring the Northern Reaches to Kendal are nothing if not ambitious. The eight locks at Tewitfield would require new

The stable restored as a store for the Canal Trust's tripboat, moored alongside, 2008.

gates and gear, and tunnel-like bridges would replace seven culverts, three of them under the M6, one of which would need a substantial diversion of the canal to gain sufficient headroom. Half-a-mile of new canal and an aqueduct would be needed to cross the A590 Kendal link road near Brettargh Holt, and onward to Kendal three new bridges, one of them an opening bridge. Further on, land sold beyond Sedgwick would have to be brought back into canal ownership. Writing in 2017, therefore, it seems on the face of it to be a very long-term project costing well into eight figures. Furthermore, Stainton aqueduct was damaged in the severe floods of December 2015, causing closure and diversion of the towing path. Stabilisation work has cost £250,000, and in August 2017 the Regeneration partnership announced that it had secured a Heritage Lottery Fund grant enabling more work to be done. The final cost of repairs has been estimated at £2.2 million, giving some indication of what total restoration to Kendal might cost.

On the other hand, elsewhere there have been some notable canal restorations which at one time were considered pipe-dreams. In particular there is the re-opening of the Rochdale Canal with 92 locks in 33 miles; its cross-Pennine companion the Huddersfield Canal with 74 in 18 miles plus a 3¼ mile-long tunnel, and a new length in Stalybridge replacing a section that had been built on; and the 57-mile long Kennet & Avon Canal with 79 locks, not to mention the remarkable Falkirk Wheel which replaces a flight of locks on the Edinburgh & Glasgow Union Canal.

All were important links forming through routes to other waterways or, in the last instance, between two important cities. Moreover, there is a precedent for restoring a canal passing under a motorway; the derelict Rochdale Canal was taken under the M62 north of Manchester, albeit that the embankment was high enough to avoid undue disturbance to motorway traffic above. The Lancaster, on the other hand, is a dead-end canal, with only a tenuous connection to the main network along the shallow, winding Ribble Link to a tidal estuary across which navigation is strictly regulated. Realistically, therefore, many millions will be needed for total restoration. So, will it happen? Stranger things have happened, not only at sea but on canals, too, and the recent voluntary restoration of 'the first furlong' at Stainton, returning it to water, is surely an indication of what can be done.

BIBLIOGRAPHY & SOURCES

My main primary sources have been the Lancaster Canal Company's minute books, extensive correspondence and plans held by the National Archive (formerly the Public Record Office) at Kew; also material at the Cumbria Archive Centre (formerly County Record Office) at Kendal, especially the Crewdson papers and the Levens mss; the Lancashire County Archives, Preston; Blackburn, Lancaster and Kendal public libraries, especially regarding the Gregson family at Lancaster; and Lancaster Maritime Museum.

Anon, *A Cursory View of the Proposed Canal from Kendal, to the Duke of Bridgewater's Canal*, n.d. but probably c1769

Anon, *Thoughts on the present design of making a Navigable Canal from the vicinity of Kendal to join some of the Canals in the South Parts of Lancashire, by way of Lancaster*, 1791 (Levens mss)

R G Armstrong, *The Rise of Morecambe (1820-1862), Trans. Hist. Socy. of Lancashire & Cheshire*, 100, 1948

Association for the Restoration of the Lancaster Canal (now Lancaster Canal Trust), *The Lancaster Canal Proposed Linear Park and Nature Reserve*, 2nd edn, c1965

E. Baines, *History, Directory, and Gazetteer of the County Palatine of Lancaster*, 1824, (reprinted as *Baines's Lancashire*, 2 vols, 1968)

P.F. Barker, *A Survey of Limekiln Sites in South Cumbria and North Lancashire*, 1997

J. Barron, *A History of the Ribble Navigation*, 1938

G. Biddle, *Lancashire Waterways*, 1980

G. Biddle, *The Lancaster Canal Tramroad, Jnl. Railway & Canal Historical Socy. IX, No. 5*, 1963

R.K. Bingham, *The Chronicles of Milnthorpe*, 1987

R.K. Bingham, *Kendal: A Social History*, 1995

C.T.G. Boucher, *John Rennie, 1761-1821*, 1963

British Waterways Board, *Cruising on the Lancaster Canal*, n.d.

A. Burton, *The Canal Builders*, 1972

M. Clarke, *The Leeds & Liverpool Canal*, 2nd edn, 2016

J.F. Curwen, *The Lancaster Canal, Trans. Cumberland & Westmorland Antiquarian & Archaeological Socy, XVII*, 1971

N. Dalziel, *Shipbuilding at Glasson Dock*, n.d.

M.D. Greville & G.O. Holt, *The Lancaster & Preston Junction Railway*, 1961

C. Hadfield, *British Canals*, 7th edn, 1984

C. Hadfield & G. Biddle, *The Canals of North West England*, 2 vols, 1970

J. Holt, *A General View of the Agriculture of the County Palatine of Lancaster*, 1794 edn.

D. Hunt, *A History of Preston*, 1992

London & North Western Railway Company, *Plans of the Lancaster Canal Navigation* (scale 2 chains : 1 inch), 1880, National Archive

Lancaster Canal Trust, *The Complete Guide to the Lancaster Canal*, 1989; 6th edn. 2017

Lancaster Canal Trust, *Fifty Years On!*, 2014

C. Nicholson, *The Annals of Kendal*, 2nd edn., 1861

R. Philpotts, *The Building of the Lancaster Canal*, 1983

J. Rigby, *The Lancaster Canal in Focus*, 2007

J. Satchell, *Kendal's Canal: History, Industry and People*, 2001

M.M. Schofield, *Outlines of the Economic History of Lancaster from 1680 to 1860*, pt.2, 1800-1860, 1951

L. Smith, *Kendal's Port, A Maritime History of the Creek of Milnthorpe*, 2009

W.E. Swale, *Sea Way to Lancaster – Glasson Dock and Sunderland Point, Past and Present*, 1977.

R. Swain, *A Walker's Guide to the Lancaster Canal*, 1990

I. Tyler, *The Gunpowder Mills of Cumbria*, 2002

A. White, (ed) *A History of Lancaster, 1193-1993*, 1993

P.N. Wilson, *Canal Head, Kendal, Trans. Cumberland & Westmorland Antiquarian & Archaeological Socy., LXVIII*, 1968

INDEX